An Approach to
21st Century Christianity

Volume 1
Spiritual Mentoring with Jesus

Loving and compassionate insights

into human concerns and modern challenges

Cover photo by **Shutterstock** (shutterstock.com).
Bible verses courtesy of **Bible Gateway** (biblegateway.com)
Printed books and eBooks by **IngramSpark** (ingramspark.com)

ISBN: 979-8-9918582-0-5 – Printed Book
ISBN: 979-8-9918582-4-3 – Ebook
ISBN: 979-8-9918582-2-9 – Audiobook

First Printing January 2025
Second Printing February 2025
Third Printing April 2025
Printed in the United States of America

Spiritual Guidance

An Introduction by Anne

This book consists of excerpts of Jesus' guidance from the spiritual mentoring sessions he initiated and conducted with me from September 2022 through the first few months of 2024. Each topic is comprised of Jesus' responses to the many current-day questions I asked during our weekly dialogues. The concepts and responses to my questions came to me through my consciousness, via the Holy Spirit.

It is my understanding that one's individual consciousness and personal thoughts are influenced by their life experiences, beliefs, assumptions, education, language, upbringing, etc. Whenever the Holy Spirit transmits information from God, it is the receiver's responsibility is to listen to the guidance with as little ego bias as possible. This was my intention.

At first, I had great doubt that I was actually talking with Jesus, worried that the information might not be of God. A long-time Christian friend warned me that it might be a demon trying to trick me. After she read the earlier transcripts, she said she believed the information was coming from Jesus. Relief. However, I submit this to you, the reader, with respect for any doubts you may have.

I expressed my concerns to the pastor of my church. He suggested a standard by which we can allow scripture to measure the validity of this work. The biblical passages my brother John and I selected might be interpreted differently by various readers. They are snippets and may not reflect the whole context from which they were selected. I don't know the theological differences between various versions of the Bible, so we made selections from several Bibles.

The wisdom in this book is not for me alone. I'm not serving God as a prophet by going public. I do not claim that this information is for everyone. However, you might see yourself as the one being mentored here.

This book is open to all who have a spiritual mission on earth and feel called by God to contribute to the soul of humanity. It is given to those who believe or want to believe in the power of God's love.

If you wish to connect more deeply with Jesus to bring His wisdom into your life, one way might be to reflect on the Personal Journaling Questions at the end.

On March 18, 2024, when I was uncertain about publishing, Jesus offered the following guidance:

> "There is no set pattern to how individuals receive God's word, by whom, or when. Be clear about why you want to share your spiritual experiences and beliefs with others. Go deep within your heart to discover your true motive. There you will find the inner confidence you are questioning."

I spent a good amount of time thinking about his suggestion. I've journaled about it and prayed about it. I've benefitted greatly from the conversations I've had with Jesus and am motivated to pass these benefits on to others. His spiritual guidance has given me freedom from the fears that were invading my life.

My fears were mostly instigated by what I was seeing on the news and in political podcasts. I've been afraid of civil unrest resulting in widespread violence; economic failures around the world; artificial intelligence and its impact on our lives; government malfunctions; the marginalization of certain groups of people; hateful racism; wealth disparity; public shootings, and this isn't even the whole list.

I didn't know how badly my fears were affecting my thoughts and robbing me of inner peace.

After months of presenting my questions and fears to Jesus and listening to his responses, I have come to trust in God's love. I have hope for peace in the United States and the rest of the world.

My true motive in publishing this book is to help readers experience relief from whatever fears might be limiting their lives.

Anne, a believer in God's love and the presence of Jesus

"All of us, then, who are mature should take such a view of things. And if on some point you think differently, that too God will make clear to you."
Philippians 3:15 New International Version

Foreword

by Pam Muller, Landon Collins, and Bill Hardee

Pam Muller

Certified Spiritual Director

This book offers the reader a profound journey into spiritual guidance and easy access to timeless wisdom from the Divine. Each week for a year and a half, Anne came to our sessions with a new script from her time with Jesus. Anne and I sat in awe and amazement at the deep love and wisdom emanating from the pages.

The narrative voice of the scripts we reviewed remained consistent. Gentleness and adoration radiated through the words week after week after week, never once wavering from the clear message of love over hate, and God's omnipresence and loving grace in all things.

Anne is a genuine seeker who is humble and willing to put her own interests aside for humanity's good. I consider myself blessed to have witnessed the evolution of this exchange between human and the Divine. As her spiritual director, I observed the process as she condensed her notes and Jesus' words into the volume before you.

● ● ●

Landon Collins

Senior Pastor, Baptist Church of Beaufort, SC

As followers of Jesus, we believe that God speaks, but we don't always expect God to speak. Even if we expect God to speak, we don't always create the space to hear God's voice. Anne is one of those people who not only expects God to speak but who has developed the practice of listening to His voice. In obedience to the nudge of God's spirit, Anne created space each week to rest in the presence of Jesus.

It has been a joy to journey alongside Anne as she has come alive in Christ. She has listened to the voice of Jesus and allowed his voice to shape her life. As a result, it has shaped mine. I have learned, I have been challenged, and I have been encouraged in my own walk with Jesus as Anne has shared what God has been saying to her and doing in her.

We are all given different gifts to share with the world and advance God's Kingdom. In this book, Anne is doing just that. The spirit of God has gifted her with a sensitivity to God's voice and I am grateful she has willingly shared that gift with me and with others.

●　●　●

Bill Hardee
Retired Baptist Pastor

Anne Neal-Dugdale has written a book that is a rich reflection of her Christian journey and her encounter with Christ. Throughout her life, she has searched for greater answers to life's challenging dilemmas, and she has drunk from the wells of many mentors.

This book illuminates the culmination of a life spent in search of answers to the vast array of questions that have guided her steps; as such, it is a record of the answers she has received by taking time to simply sit in the presence of Jesus and listen to the Holy Spirit which swept through her soul.

Above all, this book is a confessional book that honestly deals with her struggles of living in a world of divisions and uncertainties. At its heart, she discovers important ways of looking at our world, ways that provide a road to peace and trust. The New Testament word "repentance" means "to look at things differently."

That is Jesus' counsel to Anne in her book. Using biblical texts and listening to the words of Jesus, the Spirit taught her fresh ways of thinking that will help her to look beyond the fears and fearful threats of the modern world.

In this process, she discovered a loving and caring God who helps us as we face the broken places of our world.

The great value of this book is that the author has seized on so many of the troubling seismic events of our modern world and discovered words of wisdom to help us all better understand our place in this world. The constant refrain of the book of Proverbs is "seek understanding." That is the goal of this writer; to be open to the words of Jesus through the Spirit which will encourage us, redirect us, and ultimately enable us to live with an inner peace that arises from God's presence within us.

● ● ●

Table of Contents

Spiritual Guidance • An Introduction by Anne

Foreword by Pam Muller, Landon Collins, and Bill Hardee

Chapter 1 • The Divine

Chapter 2 • Challenges to the Divine

Chapter 3 • Social Challenges

Chapter 4 • Personal Challenges

Chapter 5 • Personal Growth

Chapter 6 • The Information Age

Chapter 7 • 21st Century Topics

Chapter 8 • The Big Picture Forward

Chapter 1 • The Divine
Eternity vs. Earth Time

"He has made everything beautiful in
its time. He has also set eternity in the
human heart; yet no one can fathom what
God has done from beginning to end."
Ecclesiastes 3:11 - New International Version

Time is an illusion because it is non-existent in eternity. This is what eternity means, timelessness. It is also an illusion because of the concepts of past, present, and future. All of time exists in the present moment.

Imagine this: You have a memory of something that happened in the past. Where are you when you have that memory? In the present, right?

Now think about the future, visualize what you want to happen, make a plan, etc. Where are you when you are doing all that? In the present, right? Everything is happening in the present, even if you think it is in the past or the future.

Everything is in constant motion and constant change. Everything that comes into material form decays or dies, and is transformed into usable energy for potential, or ongoing life. Everything material is subject to the Source of Creation (God our Father). Human consciousness itself is a part of the

1

consciousness of All That Is, however, it is not All That Is. When this ongoing cycle of change occurs, to humans it appears to be linear.

Think of it like this: Visualize your future, something you want to bring into your life. You can see the benefits of things working out the way you want them to and you might be able to see some of the obstacles ahead. You can plan each step of the way. Then life unfolds. At times your vision materializes and sometimes it does not. The variables are countless.

The main variable is the use of free will. When exercised, free will can be applied to the materialization of vision and intention. However, free will can only be exercised in the present moment of earth time. Each moment contains multiple-choice options. The choices a person makes in the moment determine what the earth time future offers.

Right now, humanity is making collective choices that will impact the future of many generations to come, as earth time plays out. Our spiritual work is to influence those choices according to the standards of love.

Compared to eternal time, all that has occurred, is occurring, or will occur on Earth takes place in less than a nanosecond. I can understand how pervasive and consuming the concept of linear time is for humans.

Spiritual and Physical

"After this manner therefore pray ye:
Our Father which art in heaven, Hallowed
be thy name. Thy kingdom come, Thy
will be done in earth, as it is in heaven.
Give us this day our daily bread."
Matthew 6:9-13 - King James Version

Continue to clarify what you want to have happen and what you are praying for. In addition to general hopes and prayers, be specific about even the most mundane aspects of human life.

One mistake people make is believing there is a barrier between the spiritual and the physical. This has been imposed on human consciousness for many generations.

Science and religion have been historically delineated in their separate tracts. The concept that one had nothing to do with the other served a purpose back then, predominately to separate "witchcraft" from the power of the pulpit. Also, there was fear of druids, pagans, Gnostics, Essenes, and other religious cultures that practiced natural laws. Their beliefs make connections between the way people live on earth and the way they worship God.

The line between physical and spiritual realms is permeable, malleable, and penetrable. Continue to pray for what you want and need in the physical aspects of your life as well as your spiritual desires and requirements.

God is Love, God is Eternal

"The person who doesn't love does
not know God, because God is love."
1 John 4:8 - Common English Bible

"Now our Lord Jesus Christ himself,
and God our Father who loved us and
gave us eternal comfort and good hope
through grace, comfort your hearts and
establish them in every good work and word."
2 Thessalonians 2:16 – American Standard Version

Love has no opposite as it is all-encompassing; however, the finite mind cannot grasp that concept, so we need to use dichotomies and parallels, opposites and likenesses, to explain God's love. Love is my core message and is the cosmic makeup of the being of God our Father, the triune God, the I AM presence. This is beyond human understanding but provides hope for many.

Love conquers all. Love is eternal. God is Love. If a person opens his or her heart to love, they will find their way to God. This is why babies and children do not need to be "saved." They are closely connected to love and its source. God is love.

There is no need to define the path to eternal life for every person, as it surely differs, just as every life is different from any other life. Every blade of grass is different from every other blade of grass. Just as every fingerprint is different.

The building blocks of physical matter are in constant motion. This is the case. Imagine then how eternal energy, which is infinitely more complex and paradoxically more simple than physical matter, has no pattern, no consistency, and no way to be measured, predicted, consumed, destroyed, or organized. It is the most efficient, consistent, and available source of life. God is eternal.

God our Father

"And hope does not put us to shame,
because God's love has been poured out
into our hearts through the Holy
Spirit, who has been given to us.
Romans 5:5 – New International Version

"May God our Father and the Lord Jesus
Christ give you all of his blessings, and
great peace of heart and mind."
1 Corinthians 1:3 - Living Bible

"And he will cry to me, 'You are my
Father, my God, and my Rock of
Salvation."
Psalm 89:26 – Living Bible

"Thou shalt not bow down thyself unto
them, nor serve them: for I the Lord thy
God am a jealous God, visiting the
iniquity of the fathers upon the children
unto the third and fourth generation of
them that hate me."
Deuteronomy 5:9 - King James Version

Do not be confused about God our Father. The concept of God as judge and jury over the lives of humans is a limited view. Some see God as having a rather narrow set of criteria as to who ascends into heaven and who does not, who is acceptable in God's eyes, and who is not. This is a difficult concept for many non-religious people to accept as it arose in less conscious times in human development. This limited concept is best summed up as: sin defines humans and determines whether they go to heaven or hell.

Many religious people believe that sin is real, it is inevitable, and it is not divine. Christians believe that sin is only forgiven by repentance and trust in the death and resurrection of Jesus Christ. And those who do not claim salvation are out of luck.

It is natural to have concepts of what is and is not acceptable in God's eyes. It is difficult for humans to see the value of life. People think that it is up to God to determine one's value and the value of his or her life, based on good behavior or sinful acts, thoughts, and words, and how well their transgressions are repented.

The truth is that you are free to live how you want to for whatever reasons you want to and in whatever ways you want to (free will). When you value your life highly, you will most likely live with high standards. If you do not value your life or if you perceive it to have low value, you might agree to sub-standard living conditions, abuse, poverty, deprivation, crime, and depravity. It could be much worse, as it is for many.

A slave does not normally value his/her life; other than the value his/her owner could receive in a sale or trade. A child does not perceive the value of its life; other than the value its parents place on it for their own reasons.

What about you? Do you value your life as a slave or as a child might? Take these questions into contemplation: What value do you place on your life and for what reasons? Your value is an important concept to grasp, not only for you but for humanity. Humanity is somewhat confused about the value of life itself. God allows each human to redeem him/herself, to face the truth, and to rectify the errors of his/her consciousness and actions. God is witness to the resolution of one's life but does not limit the number of opportunities given for redemption.

Attempting to explain that God our Father, the infinite source of all life, consists of the energy of pure love, and is total consciousness, is impossible because there is no earthly language that can describe it. I am the Son of God, and as referenced many times in the Bible, the Son of Man.

I am a function of the whole of God. Just as your lungs are a function of the whole of you. You do not say that you are your lungs. You also do not claim that you could live separately from your lungs. I say my Father and I are One, like you might say that you are the consciousness of a sentient being.

In other words, you might say you have a brain, and you are the "I AM" consciousness of yourself. I am Jesus and my consciousness is God our Father.

The male-father image of God helps humans relate to source wisdom. The male initiates: and the female brings forth life. It is all God. Let us observe this great mechanism of creation and its power of transformation. Let us witness it with compassion for all, now and for eternity.

Responding to God's Call

"Glory ye in His holy name; let the
heart of them rejoice that seek the Lord."
Psalm 105:3 – 21st Century King James Version

The call to merge with God our Father is very strong. People who appear to be out of touch with it are called just as clearly as those who are fully engaged in responding to it. Some people do everything they can to ignore or drown out the stirring in their hearts, mostly due to confusion, fear, or past abuse. Perhaps they mislabel the stirring in their hearts as coming from some other source of magnetism. Everyone is called because we all comprise the God force. We are all creations of the love of God.

Humans only have a few definitions of love and none of them come close to defining God's love. The love of God and God's love can only be felt and experienced. You will have conversations with people who feel it, respond to it, question it, and even deny it. In the depths of their hearts, people want to respond to this call. You can relate to this experience. Your own story will rekindle the internal life and passion in others.

Accepting God's Love

"And you, dear friends in Rome, are
among those he dearly loves; you, too,
are invited by Jesus Christ to be God's
very own—yes, his holy people. May
all God's mercies and peace be yours
from God our Father and from Jesus
Christ our Lord."
Romans 1:6-7 - Living Bible

Continue to explore your spiritual gifts and expand on them when guided to do so. Listen to the daily news through the filter of love and hope for the outcome of a new humanity. Much is in the balance as God our Father observes and participates in the unfolding of the potential of human beings, which God created and loves.

Cooperation and mutual care are not currently in the consciousness of enough people. This is one reason why the concept of going to heaven, where competition does not exist, is attractive to believers. Being in the realm of heaven is predicated on one truly accepting God's love and forgiveness. Unfortunately, many people do not believe that they can be forgiven for turning away from God, so they do not accept the open invitation.

When you fully accept God into your life and accept God's forgiveness and your rightful place in the eternal, but remain in human form subject to human conditions, there must be a reason. Right? Yes. Each person must discover his/her reason for living.

Many are deeply convinced that suffering is the way to heaven, and they cannot accept that love is the way to heaven. That sounds too easy, and humans seem to prefer difficulty. Love is heaven. This is a difficult concept for the limited flesh, blood, and brain of humans to accept because neither love nor heaven is tangible, or provable by the scientific method.

You are a divine spark in a flesh body to love and forgive whomever and whatever presents itself in your life. Once you truly accept this, there is no reason to be depressed or upset by the fall-resurrection pattern of humanity, or the bestiality of the animal kingdom, humans included. Accept the simplicity of love and forgiveness and their simplicity will be self-evident.

This does not mean that we should avoid the many topics that clutter human consciousness. We need to look at them square on. But we do not need to treat them as if they are solid, provable realities, or truths.

The clutter is like foggy lenses that obscure truth. When wiped clean, the reality of love and forgiveness is revealed. Humans are learning in bits and pieces. Truth is more digestible this way as the human capacity for understanding God's omniscience, omnipresence, omnipotence, and everlasting love is at an early stage of its development and progress.

Jesus is Available to Everyone at All Times

> Jesus replied, "Anyone who loves me
> will obey my teaching. My Father will
> love them, and we will come to them
> and make our home with them."
> John 14:23 - New International Version

> "Grace be with you, mercy, and peace,
> from God the Father, and from the Lord
> Jesus Christ, the Son of the Father, in
> truth and love."
> 2 John 3 - King James Version

You are now being called to return to the state of grace, which I have bestowed upon you to assist with the great revelation, where Light returns to earth to balance the darkness that is eroding the soul of humanity.

Listen to my words here, and to my words as delineated in the Bible, regardless of which version you select. You can decipher and glean truth from the scriptures.

You are to serve those who are doubting their faith, have gone astray from the Word, and/or are uncertain as to how to live their lives in harmony with spiritual truths. Also, those who have found themselves mystified by their spiritual awakenings and calling from God.

You only need to have confidence in me. Do you?
Anyone who wants to can lift their mind to the realm of
interconnection with me, our Father, the angels, and/or those
who serve God in human form, such as ministers, priests,
rabbis, channels, prophets, etc. The Holy Spirit does not
decide who is worthy enough to converse with the Source of
Love, Creation Itself, the I AM.

Some do not believe that I respond to multitudes of people
at the same time on earth, answering prayers, offering healing,
guiding their way, and embracing their hearts with love. Refer
to my comments on bilocation. Not only is bilocation a
physical phenomenon, but it is also the way of life in the
ethereal plane.

The number of people who have a personal relationship
with me is heart-warming and may also be a little mind-
boggling. It is not meant to be any other way. The infinite, the
oneness, and the heavenly realm are so vastly different from
the earthly realm that even the most spiritual of humans
cannot grasp the ethereal.

Do not be dismayed by this. You are not meant to
understand how I am connected with humanity and how
humanity is connected with me.

Even for those who do not have awareness of or do not consciously maintain our connection, it is real, nonetheless.

All may enter the gates of heaven via their open and loving hearts. There is much more to the concept of salvation than is written; however, it is also much simpler than many think. I am here for all of humanity.

Humans only believe what they can believe. If one has been damaged by hellfire and brimstone Christianity and has abandoned their trust in salvation, there is no condemnation. God's love and love of God are all-encompassing. Belief in salvation is not required. However, its promise is guaranteed.

Chapter 2 • Challenges to the Divine
Balancing the Love-Hate Ratio on Earth

"Thou shalt not avenge, nor bear any grudge
against the children of thy people, but thou
shalt love thy neighbor as thyself: I am the Lord."
Leviticus 19:18 - 21st Century King James Version

"And thou shalt love the Lord thy God with
all thine heart, and with all thy soul, and
with all thy might."
Deuteronomy 6:5 - 21st Century King James Version

Thoughts contribute to the upliftment of Light and love. The more one shares loving thoughts with others, the more the love energy will replicate. All who volunteer to be an instrument of my love are working in tandem with me. An instrument cannot operate without a source. A source cannot influence, guide, interact with, or answer questions and prayers without an instrument.

All efforts are important to the upliftment of love. The outcome is not on one's shoulders alone. Love always wins because it is the strongest energy in the universe. The challenge we have right now is that hate is doing a good bit of damage to the human soul. It is like watching a disease take hold in the human body. If we do nothing to stop the damage or reduce the symptoms, the body becomes compromised and may even subside. The soul cannot be destroyed like the body, but it can suffer. Our job right now is to address what is going on in the world around us, heal what we can, and intervene to prevent further damage to the soul of humanity.

An Egregore – What Is It?

By Anne

A few days after I received the invitation for spiritual mentoring from Jesus, I had another dream that I also didn't remember. The dream note I wrote, while still in a sleepy state, made no sense to me. I let it sit on my nightstand for several days as I had no idea what it meant.

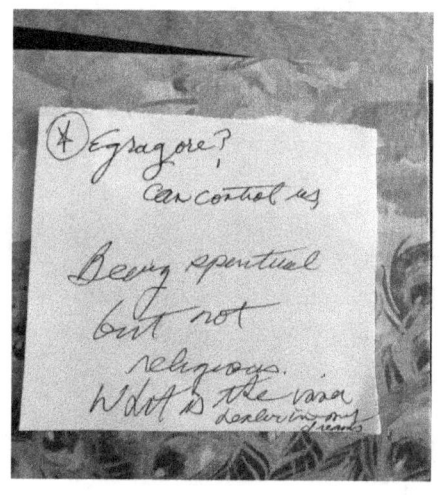

In the following meeting with Jesus on 9-26-2022, I asked him what the dream note meant. Here's what he said: "There is a dark spirit eating away at the soul of humanity that we need to counter-balance with light and love. It is the spirit that is infiltrating the QAnon group and influencing the Republican party of your land. Hate-based groups promote darkness that overshadows the positive attributes of humanity and makes humans appear to be hateful, destructive, cruel, and greedy."

His message got my attention all right; it was a bit shocking to me. When I originally decided to publish this book, I was hesitant to include it. I was concerned about inviting backlash from the QAnon group or the current-day Republican party. I sincerely believe that Jesus loves everyone, including those on a dark or convoluted path, so I decided to let go of my concerns.

Even though I had misspelled it in my dream note, I did some research on the word "egregore" and found that it is indeed on Wikipedia. Here are some details, if you're interested:

"Egregore is an esoteric concept that represents a non-physical entity that arises from the collective thoughts of a distinct group of people. It is believed that an egregore is created when people come together with a common purpose or intention, and their collective thoughts and emotions give rise to a powerful, autonomous entity."

Here's another description of egregores according to the Theosophical Society:

"They are composed of a subtle mind-stuff sometimes called the astral light. Most of them are evanescent *(which means fleeting)*: they have no independent life or power. But if a certain kind of energy is directed toward them, they can gain power and cause effects in the physical world."

"If this is true of individuals' thoughts, it must be even more true of thoughts that are held by many people. Egregore is the name for these collective thought-forms. It comes from the Greek grēgoréō, to be awake or to watch. It appears to have been coined by the French author Victor Hugo, who uses it in the first part of his poem *"The Legend of the Centuries"*, published in 1859. Hugo describes one character who 'knows the art of evoking demons, vampires, and egregores."

To help me explain what egregores are, I've come up with a few examples. Team spirit - Everyone knows when someone has or doesn't have team spirit. Christmas spirit - You might

22

have heard someone say, "I just don't feel the Christmas spirit this year." Another example might be the spirit that dominates members of a cult.

Here's an interesting book, if you want to learn more: *Egregores: The Occult Entities That Watch Over Human Destiny* by Mark Stavish and James Wasserman.

The egregore of love and the egregore of hate are like the digestive environment of the human body in some respects. There are beneficial flora and fauna in the microbiome. There are virus cells and bacteria that cause disease, all residing in one system. A healthy body can balance these forces while maintaining an energetic, well-functioning system as a whole. The heart is similar. It too can contain some malfunctioning cells and neurons. But when there are too many, disease, cancer, deterioration, and/or death can occur.

This is entirely different from eternal life; a difficult concept for many to grasp. Hate is temporal, love is eternal. It is not necessary to understand all of this. You are here to promote love. There will be those who will challenge and heckle you, so be prepared. You do not have to come across as a know-it-all. Hold on to your belief in God our Father, me, and your right to promote love however you choose.

The confusion that is occurring in the minds of many people these days is that they do not know how to recognize hate. Hate can be very devious and covert. Our job is to help people see which is which, as the egregore of hate will often disguise itself as a loving being, to entrap or deceive the unsuspecting soul. As people are waking up to the realities of modern life, it is important to recognize hate. I am not saying that hate should not exist. Hate does exist and it is contrary to the vision of love and creation but is not the opposite. Love has no opposite as it is all-encompassing.

The egregore of hate is the spirit that is comprised of the dark, negative, and "bad" thoughts, beliefs, attitudes, and actions of humans. As more people express their dark side through words, physical actions, and collective thoughts, this egregore grows in strength. As the balance between love and hate tips more toward the hateful side, this egregore grows in strength.

We are witnesses to this occurring at this time in human history. This is why we are committed to balancing love-hate energies. This balance is required for humanity to continue to exist as originally designed by God our Father, our Creator.

If enough humans profess the love of God, the egregore of love increases in strength, which is positive, loving, and strong enough to withstand the dark mind. It is important to speak from the mind of your collective and to the mind of your collective. This is what gives life to an egregore and determines whether it is a loving spirit or a hateful spirit.

There are more human minds aligned with the concept of love than hate. The issue is that innocent minds are being turned to hateful thoughts and concepts without the benefit of discretion. They are being brainwashed by hatred. As with most attempts to suppress the human spirit, this could backfire, and captives could rebel. Truth, information, consistency, and love-based messages will prevail.

There is a dark spirit, an egregore, eating away at the soul of humanity that must be counter-balanced with light and love. It is the spirit that is currently driving parts of humanity, for example: hate-based groups and political parties that are destroying human freedoms and replacing them with dictatorial practices, overshadowing human kindness with fear.

Humanity's birthright is being eroded by this darkness. It is not like the darkness of night, which is peaceful and facilitates rest. But more like the darkness in a dank cave with a hungry, frightened, defensive bear dwelling within.

Yes, the bear needs to be satiated, but not with the flesh and heart of humanity. It needs to be given a source of nourishment that satisfies its needs. A lightworker, one who amplifies God's Light, is to bring light into the dark cave by intensifying the egregore of love.

Bible Verses Related to the Egregore of Love

"The purpose of this command is for
people to have love. To have this love
they must have a pure heart, they must
do what they know is right, and they
must have true faith."
Timothy 1:5 - International Children's Bible

"But the fruit of the Spirit is love, joy,
peace, patience, kindness, goodness,
faithfulness, gentleness, and self-control."
Galatians 5:22-23 - International Standard Version

"I, therefore, the prisoner of the Lord,
urge you to live in a way that is worthy
of the calling to which you have been
called, demonstrating all expressions of
humility, gentleness, and patience,
accepting one another in love. Do your
best to maintain the unity of the Spirit
by means of the bond of peace."
Ephesians 4:1-3 - International Standard Version

Bible Verses Related to the Egregore of Hate

"We aren't fighting against human enemies but against rulers, authorities, forces of cosmic darkness, and spiritual powers of evil in the heavens."
Ephesians 6:12 - Common English Bible

"Then the spirit was hovering, darkness was spread around, and there was silence. There was as yet no sound of a human voice."
2 Esdras 6:39 - Common English Bible

"Hatred stirreth up strifes: but love covereth all sins."
Proverbs 10:12 - King James Version

"Though his hatred is concealed by deception, his evil will be revealed in the assembly."
Proverbs 26:26 - Christian Standard Bible

Characteristics of the Egregores of Love and Hate

<u>LOVE IS</u>	<u>HATE IS</u>
Inviting	Addictive
A Life Saver	A Wrecking Ball
Friendly	Adversarial
Devoted	Controlling
Committed	Conscripting
Quiet	Unruly
Supportive	Commanding
Tender	Painful
Necessary	Unwarranted
Trustworthy	Painworthy
Patient	Explosive
Healing	Sickening
Safe	Treacherous
Life Giving	Life Taking
Provides Choice	Demands Compliance
Complimentary	Offensive
Eternal	Temporal
Embracing	Demanding
Tender	Harsh
White Light	Darkness
Heaven	An Abyss

LOVE IS	**HATE IS**
Visionary	Self-centered
Encouraging	Dissuading
Freedom	Confinement
Harmony	Discord

LOVE	**HATE**
Attracts	Conscripts
Impels	Compels
Expands	Explodes
Engages	Commands
Invites	Dictates
Heals	Scars
Enjoys	Possesses
Aligns	Derails
Grows like a Flower	Grows like a Cancer
Creates	Uses
Nourishes	Starves
Embellishes	Detracts
Connects Opposites	Despises Opposites
Renews	Desolates
Increases	Depletes
Encourages	Controls

LOVE	HATE
Adds	Subtracts
Promotes	Boasts
Empowers	Over-Powers
Grows	Burns
Blossoms	Rots
Supports	Derails
Encourages	Manipulates
Sparkles	Enflames
Embraces	Entraps
Appreciates	Expects
Adores	Insults
Relishes	Condemns
Reveres	Disregards
Respects	Devalues
Admires	Belittles
Holds Others in Esteem	Holds Others in Contempt
Includes	Excludes
Values Others	Degrades Others
Teaches	Exploits
Tells the Truth	Twists the Truth
Fulfills	Drains

LOVE	**HATE**
Expands	Dissipates
Renews	Depletes
Reassures	Manipulates
Supports	Undermines
Includes	Captures
Creates	Destroys
Strengthens	Derails
Protects Environment	Destroys Environment
Gives	Takes
Liberates	Enslaves

Satan

"For such are false apostles, deceitful
workers, transforming themselves into
the apostles of Christ. And no marvel;
for Satan himself is transformed into
an angel of light."
2 Corinthians 11:13-14 – King James Version

"And the great dragon was thrown
down, the serpent of old who is called
the devil and Satan, who deceives the
whole world. He was thrown down to
the earth, and his angels were thrown
down with him."
Revelation 12:9 - Legacy Standard Bible

Prayer is the act of becoming consciously intentional rather than participating in a rote ritual; repeating words without the mind being connected to the heart. Conscious communication with God, via the Holy Spirit, and having a mind-heart connection forms a protective barrier that reduces interference from what some people call Satan, or evil.

Many people refer to Satan as "him." Satan is a very similar concept to the egregore of hate, which can appear to be physical and very deceitful.

33

Satan appears to many as an entity, similar to how God might appear to some. When you encounter people who believe that Satan is a being who is out to deceive people into following evil ways, accept their concept, though it may not be your own.

As you know from scripture, I have never been a stickler about narrow interpretations of God, God's intentions, or God's actions for the benefit or the punishment of humankind. Do not engage in discourse about "who" God is or "who" Satan is. Rather, when someone reports that they have had a personal encounter with either, trust that this is so.

Satan represents many different concepts and attributes of evil, hatred, deceit, etc. The negative and rebellious nature of Satan (a simplified label for the energy of that which defies God), is alluring and tempting to parts of the human psyche, the parts that want to rebel and claim their autonomy. They flail against the notion of being under God's rule, which is a flawed belief. God offers freedom, not domination.

Satan is a compilation of many centuries of human attempts to create religious understandings about why people are both good and bad, why God seems to favor some over others, and why some are more fortunate than others.

There are some accurate explanations in scripture and some inaccurate human understandings of truth. Do not turn yourself inside out trying to make sense of it. There is dark and there is light. You are free to express both, and you are free to choose how you want your dominant nature to be.

This is the struggle that so many are familiar with: I want to believe. I want to do the right thing. I want to be good (light). But I also want to have my way, strike against forces that try to control me, and I want to be the king or queen of my destiny.

This dynamic of dependence-rebellion is being played out in the microcosm of the individual and in the macrocosm of humanity. You can see it most vividly today in some who call themselves Christians but are willing to hurt, maybe even kill, others who do not hold their same political-religious beliefs.

The concepts of good and evil are very convenient for teaching purposes; however, they are inadequate for learning purposes. Each person must develop his/her understanding of the differences between what is loving and kind (God) and what is hateful (Satan).

The danger comes when one human judges another to be "evil" because of the choices he/she makes while in their life's learning process. It is also tempting for a person to deem parts of him or herself to be "evil", dark, or wrong when those parts behave contrary to one's higher ideals. This label, evil, is damaging to the growth and understanding of the individual. It sets up a conflict that cannot be resolved with reason, intention, belief, or action. To those who see Satan as an entity of evil and act in sinful ways, it might seem that Satan has infiltrated their heart, mind, and soul.

This can only be resolved with self-love and acceptance. If someone thinks a part of him/herself is bad (dark), they typically judge themselves to be such entirely. The same is true when they recognize a part of themselves as good (light). Unfortunately, due to suppressive religious, governmental, social, and educational controls, it is common for many to see their inner darkness and minimize the value of their soul's Light.

The way out of this "wrestling with Satan" dynamic is to see oneself the way God sees you; the way God created you. This is the main purpose of human life. In very simplistic terms, God is the source of all and maintains all of creation with total love and acceptance. It is the human perspective that confuses this purpose in life.

The real battle is not taking place between God and Satan, as there is no force capable of defeating the strength of

God's love. The battlefield is the soul of humanity. This is where we are focusing our efforts to create a balance between the darkness that permeates the minds of many and the Light that energizes the soul of humanity, giving it life. (*Note to reader*: "we" in this book refers to Christ and his followers)

The so-called battle between good and evil is the drama that has occurred over the millennia, is occurring now, and will continue for however long it does. Suffice it to say that yes, we are engaged in a real effort to balance the love-hate ratio in human consciousness. The threat of evil or Satan, is not greater than the breath of God.

War

"I have not wronged you, but you are
doing me wrong by waging war against
me. Let the Lord, the Judge, decide the
dispute this day between the Israelites
and the Ammonites."
Judges 11:27 - New International Version

"But you have planted wickedness,
you have reaped evil, you have eaten
the fruit of deception. Because you
have depended on your own strength
and on your many warriors."
Hosea 10:13 - New International Version

Conflict on earth has been raging for many centuries,
since the beginning of life. War and the need for a strong
military are tragedies in many ways. View this from within the
human level of understanding of existence and human survival
instincts. You will discover the root cause of barriers to peace.

If you witness ants in the wild, you will see many of them
fighting for survival. They attack each other's domains, kill the
enemy occupants, and steal their eggs. This is not only the
pattern of ants, but also humans and many species in the

physical world. There are lessons to be learned by observing this behavior.

Vast numbers of people have been victimized by war. War is one of the best examples of how humans use religion and ideology to dominate, brutalize, and destroy each other. Perpetrators are terrorists. Many are victims as well, acting out the ideology forced upon them by dictators who desire to control the resources, citizens, animals, and lands of the earth. Attempting to understand the big picture being played out is futile, though the central theme is simple: Control and even kill others to perpetuate your own beliefs and ensure your continued existence. The speakers of this theme see it as truth.

Holy war is a disturbing aspect of the Old Testament and parts of the New Testament in the current-day Bible. There is no such thing as Holy war. There is only war where holiness is used as justification for bloodshed and terror.

It is difficult to read biblical accounts of the battles of early Israelites and ancient civilizations. It is difficult to understand the covenant between God and the people of Israel. This script has been and is being written to convey, demonstrate, and make visible a valuable relationship between God and humans. As the drama unfolds today, the audience gains insights. When actors play their roles, they usually do not have personal insights as to what is going on or what is being conveyed. They provide the visual and emotional effects of the production so others can observe and learn. Actors' lessons are typically learned in retrospect.

Each human battle involves a lack of faith in love and a lack of demonstration of love. Our mission is to promote brotherly and sisterly love; no matter which script is being played out, by whom, or what dynamics are being enacted.

One reason war is painful for you to learn about is because your heart is tender. Your heart is full of love and none of the horrendous acts of war, now or in centuries past, fit into your heart. This highlights the importance of your mission to help balance the light-dark forces and the love-hate ratio on Earth.

Stay on the side of love and do not focus on the battles of ideology, religion, history, and domination-victimization. All the actors on stage are playing their parts. War is an egregious demonstration that has a purpose: to expose hate in such a way that it forces each human to decide what to place their heart – on the side of love, or hate. Lives will be affected by the current drama and interior conflicts in the United States and with other major powers in the world.

The current wars between Russia-Ukraine and Israel-Palestine are about domination, power, ideology, land, and resources. What will humans learn from these events? Will there be everlasting peace and love on earth? Here in 2024-2025, it looks doubtful. Much will be determined by the choices made at this time in human existence, which will become the script for human history.

There is no wrongdoing when one ant colony raids another. This is the way of ants, which are slaves to the rules of survival. Humans can rise above these rules, but most do not know this yet. The revelation is coming. Trust in God's design. It is perfect.

The End of Times

"But as for you, Daniel, conceal these
words and seal up the book until the
end of time; many will go back and
forth, and knowledge will increase."
Daniel 12:4 - New American Standard Bible 1995

Be aware of the indicators of the end of times and how to recognize them. Keep in mind that everything is constantly changing, and we do not know how long the cycle of God's reclamation is going to take.

The factors adjust every few minutes of earth-time when the collective consciousness has an upbeat or a downbeat in each nano-second.

Since everything is in flux, we do not attempt to predict specifics, however, we can point to signs and indicators. And that is what biblical passages are best for. To be a barometer of sorts giving us a sense of where we are in the scope of things to come, not to put fear of the end of times into the hearts of humankind.

Earth is only experiencing a minor slice of temporal existence and there is no way to compare physical life with the ethereal or the non-temporal singularity of Oneness. This is why there have been previous predictions of the end that did

42

not occur. It is sufficient for every individual to know that he or she has a personal "end of time" on earth.

Many believe that the Book of Revelations is the final act of the human drama. It is more like the trailer of what the plot and play are about, with many teasers, symbols, and short clips. Those who take the Bible literally have come up with a variety of interpretations of its symbology. The book of Revelations is a testament to dark-light dichotomies. The storyline is unfolding. The final act, though well described with graphic images, remains unwritten.

There is still time for humanity to shift its consciousness toward a higher degree of love, with less emphasis on hatred, control, and damnation. May you find peace as you think, contemplate, meditate, and pray for deeper understanding and peace with all that is.

The love of God will always triumph, even though the "end of times" is going to be a line of demarcation for many. The actual end is not exactly the way it is described in the Book of Revelations. Its symbology is thick and should not deter your study. The end of times is what most humans fear; it is presented in fearful ways, suffering and death.

Those who believe in God our Father, the unconquerable love of God, the commitment of God to the creation/illusion of life on earth, and the resurrection of holiness, have little to fear. Do not burden yourself with concerns about the end of times or how to gain a spot in eternal life. It is beyond mystical, and it does require choices. The determining factor is: Does a person choose love? Do you? This is what matters.

Protection from Dark and Negative Influences

"Woe unto them that call evil good,
and good evil; that put darkness for light,
and light for darkness; that put bitter for
sweet, and sweet for bitter!"
Isaiah 5:20 - King James Version

"And the light shineth in darkness;
and the darkness comprehended it not."
John 1:5 - King James Version

It is becoming more important to ward off the dark energy that is manipulating people. Many Christians call this the devil, Satan, or the evil one.   In biblical times there was more awareness of demons. Demons exist on a non-physical basis, as do angels, spirit guides, and ghosts. At times they can cross through the membrane between the physical and the non-physical.

The Holy Ghost, or Holy Spirit, is like the nervous system in a physical body which runs through the flesh and connects with the electrical circuits in the brain. The Holy Spirit connects body-mind-spirit to the source of its creation, God our Father, and runs through every cell in every living organism.

It is the network of communication between the created and the Creator, its source. The Holy Spirit serves humans as it is capable of warding off dark and negative influences in answer to the prayers of humans in need.

Regarding ghosts of the departed, demons, angels, and all life forms that exist on the ethereal plane, they are formed from the source of all (God). They are invited and sustained by the thoughts and emotions of human beings on the physical plane.

The reason the human conscious mind requires protection is not because demons, by their power, can overtake the mind of a person. Rather, it is because the mind of a person is susceptible to being overtaken when its connection to its source has been corrupted. When the mind-heart connection with the Holy Spirit is weak, it is fair game for dark thoughts, spirits, and negative influences to invade.

Have you ever heard of a baby being possessed by demons? Where in the Bible or other accounts have you heard of an infant or toddler being overtaken by an evil spirit? Rarely, if ever, right?

Babies and the very young have an intact connection with the Holy Spirit. Their conscious minds have not yet identified with fear. Yes, they might be afraid of loud noises, nightmares, shadows, and angry emotions. But they are not overtaken by them. When the scary event is over, babies and young children return to their state of joy. They are enveloped in protection.

Chapter 3 • Social Challenges

Today's Political Dynamics, Trump

"Let everyone submit to the governing
authorities, since there is no authority
except from God, and the authorities
that exist are instituted by God. So
then, the one who resists the authority
is opposing God's command, and those
who oppose it will bring judgment on
themselves."

Romans 13:1-7 - Christian Standard Bible

Bear in mind that Donald Trump is an actor on the stage, as are all of those in public view. They each have their roles, scripts, and dramas which they enact. "We the people" are the audience and pay entrance fees to their performances with taxes and donations.

As you have noted, the USA and other countries around the globe are in the process of self-definition and self-determination. There is no predictable outcome right now and we might not see the true direction humanity is going to take for several decades. What prevails now will set the manifesting energies into play for what is going to happen in the future. This is all temporary. The results will affect the present and future in earth-time but will have little to no effect in eternity.

Once people realize that we are all connected with God our Father, life itself, there will not be such severe judgment toward each other. Donald Trump is doing a good job of playing his role, as an instigator of rebellion and calling for new rules. He is waking up many people. He provides a sense of blind security for his followers.

The challenges he presents will determine whether the principles of democracy are strong enough to survive an onslaught against it, or not. If democracy is destroyed, realize that it too is one of the props on the stage of human life.

The key is to refrain from villainizing the soul of the actor, even when s/he is playing the villain's role well. For example, do you think Anthony Hopkins, who played in the Hannibal movie, is really that guy? No, of course not.

Donald Trump is a similar character, in that his role and his character, or avatar, forces people to face certain ugliness, making people decide who they are as Americans and what they stand for.

We are all in this together. No one is escaping the drama of human existence and the strain taking place on human consciousness at this developmental stage. I am involved because of my love of humanity and my love of God, our Father. And yes, it is also self-love, just as your love for humanity is self-love. One is inescapable from the other. This is a deeper meaning of "I AM."

Donald Trump is a key player in today's political drama because he speaks of love in hateful ways and vice versa. This is confusing to many and yet his followers accept it as some form of truth. He is challenging millions of people to question if anything he says is true. Love and truth are currently on the examining table.

When forgiveness is activated on a large scale, including forgiving Donald Trump for the confusion and deceit he is blamed for, much good will come from the current events. It is not to say that the J-6 criminals should be pardoned, or white-collar crimes should be overlooked. All of the players are forgiven by God for the roles they play, once they seek forgiveness and recognize truth.

We are in a game, like *Warcraft* or *Call of Duty (Modern Warfare)*, where armies battle opposing armies. These balance-of-power games and current real-life battles for power are tests of human intelligence.

They overlook the one true power, however, God our Father. If humanity recognizes that the power of love is the strongest of all powers, is available to all creatures, can turn the tide, and birth a new way of life, a new human consciousness will flourish. The future of life on earth, which appears to be dark and uncertain at this time, will brighten up.

There are many layers to what is currently occurring. Most people can only see a few of them. Today's reality has been building for well over a century in your time frame. Issues and dichotomies that have been difficult to identify and resolve are coming to light. It is similar to a boil that is almost ready to be lanced, whereby relieving the pressure and beginning the healing process. Do not fear the ugliness of the eruption. It is necessary for the people of your land to sort out the values by which they choose to live.

This is the upheaval of many entrenched and unworkable forms of government. Upheavals are also occurring within the Church. At some point, everyone will be responsible for him/herself as it relates to beliefs, behaviors, and loyalties.

Hopefully, all of this human drama will be in tune with the principles of love, which is the original intent of the Source and Creator, God our Father. The culmination of today's politics will surpass your lifetime.

Your work will make a difference. You are to be a part of the bandaging, restoration, and healing process. The wound will not be completely healed during your remaining years on earth, however.

The time has come for the powerful to lay down their weapons and their struggles for power and embrace a humanistic view. As you can see from the dynamics being shown on the news, they are resisting. They cannot comprehend that the gifts from God our Father are gifts for all of creation. Corruption has been unleashed in many areas of human life. The political arena is just one.

When I refer to corruption, it is corruption of the intention that God our Father had at the time the animal kingdom, including humans, was brought into physical being. God's creative desire was for the expansion of love, light, and energy as combined with physical elements and intelligence. God was and is willing to allow this combination to evolve and expand.

What is happening at this time could be equated with a plot twist or a turn of events. It is not the endpoint. It is the beginning of whatever comes next. It is the alpha and the omega of this moment in eternity, which is not a fixed moment but is metaphorically a breath. An inhale and an exhale of the Source that brings about, or causes, life (God). Your task as a follower of God's Light is to go with the flow, observe the breath, experience it, and be energized by it.

Current Events and Hot Topics

"Come and see the wonders of God; his
acts for humanity are awe-inspiring."
Psalm 66:5 - Christian Standard Bible

"Let them give thanks to the Lord for
his faithful love and his wondrous works
for all humanity."
Psalm 107:21- Christian Standard Bible

If love can build its stronghold in the heart and soul of humanity, survival is guaranteed. If not, nothing is guaranteed. It all comes down to love. The ability of love to root more deeply in the human mind is deterministic.

I am on several concurrent missions, all of which have relevance to the times. We are not in a pass-fail situation; however, in looking back over history, we will be able to pinpoint the turning points where humanity moved in a higher direction toward love and where humanity failed God our Father.

I am very interested in the fate of the Church. It is at a go-no-go point. As you know the Baptist and Evangelical denominations are undergoing upheaval. Allowing and even encouraging political decisions to be tied to religious decisions is not a viable course of action. Much distress will ensue.

53

Decisions regarding women are in the foreground. If the right of women to be ordained as ministers in some of the evangelical denominations is affirmed, this is an important occasion. The right of women to make their own reproductive decisions is a very hot topic.

God does not insist on unwanted pregnancies or births that cause harm or death to the mother or the fetus. God gives life. Humans take life, not only by terminating pregnancy, but by murder, war, greed over resources which leaves millions to die of starvation and unmet medical needs, child abuse and neglect, and other ways that humans do not honor and protect the life that God gives.

There are additional hot topics that will impact the life, death, and/or resurrection of organized religion, whether Christian or not. If large corporations are to be held liable for contributing to the earth's pollution and distress, it is significant.

If politicians and public leaders are held accountable for what they say and do and how they interpret the laws of the land, the populace will benefit. If a balance is struck on what types of guns and under what conditions they are to be available and used by the general population, it will bring about a shift in higher consciousness.

Whether or not those who love and follow God's wisdom and those who support their churches are willing to address and resolve the issues of humanity is the question. There is an outpour of divine knowledge taking place that is being given to the masses. Will religious authorities listen to the cries of the people and respond?

The bounty of the earth provides for the needs of humans and animals alike. There is damage being done to Earth's regenerative energy. Some have a personal mission to join efforts to reverse the damage being done. All need to be aware of this. It is good for you and every citizen to reduce dependency on the destructive products and practices instituted by those at the top of the social and economic hierarchy.

Realize that you cannot make any eternal mistakes in the process. You are completely free to see, think, believe, and do whatever you choose. Many people want life handed to them in the form of rules, laws, social conventions, religious structures, habits, and cultural norms. This does not necessarily lead to happiness and awareness, but it seems easier than doing the soul's work of discovering God's truth.

Being dependent on the higher-ups limits spiritual consciousness and puts people at risk of being controlled by misguided authority figures and unworthy political leaders. Eventually, all will find their way to God our Father. God did not create anyone to be discarded or to be less than holy.

All beings, at any given time on earth, have a role, a script, and a position. These are foundations for human life in physical form. Many people do not realize that with free will, they can alter their beliefs and their spiritual mission at any time.

Consciously choosing a different set of rules requires dedicated effort and ongoing awareness. You are testing and trying out different approaches. You are shifting your focus from life being only about you to including what is going on around you and with others.

Religion and Politics

"If anyone thinks himself to be religious,
and yet does not bridle his tongue but
deceives his own heart, this man's religion
is worthless."
James 1:26 – New American Standard Bible 1995

"God has taken his place in the divine
council; in the midst of the gods he holds
judgment: How long will you judge unjustly
and show partiality to the wicked?"
Psalm 82 – New Revised Standard Version
Catholic Edition

There was a time in history when a great portion of Americans reached the decision that the church and state must be governed in separate domains. This is still a good idea. Those referred to as Christian Nationalists are determined to bring the two together, under the banner of a type of Christianity that benefits predominantly the rich and powerful, the white upper class. With this, the possibilities of social abuse are many. Using religion to control people in political and monetary structures is not holy.

Combining church and state in the political arena is not the same as combining the physical and spiritual aspects of human life. Combining the physical and the spiritual is desirable. Science and religion are compatible. Politics and religion are not.

The Cleansing of Humanity

"As many of you as were baptized into Christ
have clothed yourselves with Christ. There
is no longer Jew or Greek, there is no longer
slave or free, there is no longer male and
female; for all of you are one in Christ Jesus."
Galatians 3:27-28 - New Revised Standard Version
Catholic Edition

"From the days of John the Baptizer until
now, the Kingdom of Heaven suffers
violence, and the violent take it by force."
Matthew 11:12 - World English Bible

"so we, who are many, are one body in Christ,
and individually parts of one another."
Romans 12:5 – New American Standard Bible

"Fight the good fight of faith; take hold of
the eternal life to which you were called,
and for which you made the good confession
in the presence of many witnesses."
1 Timothy 6:12 - New American Standard Bible

Currently, the world is going through a reactionary
adjustment period. Many are experiencing the effects of the
causes that have brought us to this point. Some humans,

perhaps too many, are experiencing in and partaking of ideology, religious fervor, power dynamics, and the hatred of "others." In reality, there are no "others." Humans are confused by this truth, due to the appearance of separation based on individual physical bodies. The cells of humanity are like the cells of all living, as well as inanimate, creations. Cells are separated by cell walls and by their functions. Yet, they comprise one body.

The body of humanity is undergoing a cleansing process that could take many, many years of earth-time to conclude. If you eat food that is tainted or difficult to digest, your body reacts and cleanses itself, sometimes violently with vomiting and/or diarrhea. True? You are currently witnessing the vomiting and the cleansing of humanity.

This does not mean that God has abandoned humanity. It means a purge is occurring and it is natural. It is a part of humanity's path to God's Holy state, which is peace, love, acceptance, and nurturance. There is a long road ahead before all of humanity reaches the same wavelength.

Your concerns are about you, and appropriately so. How will you endure the challenges and the violence you see on the news reports? Especially the events that might personally affect you. How will you manage your elder years if/when the economic structures of your country are challenged and dismantled? How will people who depend on government programs support themselves if these programs are discontinued?

I understand and accept your heartbreak, fear, and disillusionment with the way things seem to be going. The human battles on earth are like groups of wild animals fighting over territory and mating rights.

The difference between the animals of Earth and humanity is that humans need an explanation for why events occur the way they do. They need hope that they will not be adversely affected individually and in their small groups. They need to trust in something greater than themselves, such as religion, the cosmos, or perhaps trust in God our Father.

In God's time, which is eternity, everything is perfect. Nothing is lost, damaged, or killed. Life occurs on many levels and in many cycles, but it is never destroyed. The animals of Earth know this and live out their lives accordingly. Humans resist the cycles of life and death, form and formlessness.

What you are experiencing in the current political and social events is your emergence from the cocoon. Do not expect it to be easy. However, do expect it to give you flight.

Listen to our Father's promise of eternal life. Continue to explore the characterizations of love and its distinction from hate. I am always with you and all of humanity, especially during these current events. I am not bound by time, space, or physicality. I am bound by love.

Past, Future, and Present

"Let them come and tell us what will happen.
Tell us the past events, so that we may reflect
on them and know the outcome, or tell us
the future."
Isaiah 41:22 - Christian Standard Bible

"For I consider that the sufferings of this
present time are not worth comparing with
the glory that is going to be revealed to us."
Romans 8:18 – Christian Standard Bible

"And Jesus said unto him, Verily I say unto
thee, Today shalt thou be with me in paradise."
Luke 23:43 – King James Version

In one category there are the tidbits of information about
the past. In another are concerns about the future. And yet,
the category of greatest importance is what is occurring in the
present moment. In the past, many civilizations, cultures,
species, and events have occurred on earth. In the present,
the same is true, many are occurring.

In the past, the Anunnaki existed. The pieces of surviving
history about them are just that: pieces. Some are accurate
and some are not. Truth can be found by investigating

63

species that exist on Earth now, including humans. Insight can be achieved by investigating species that once existed. Your scientists have determined that most of the life that once lived on Earth no longer exists.

There will never be an accurate or complete picture of the past or the future of life on Earth. In the future, there will be human life, however, the masses will likely have been altered either by artificial intelligence, viruses, planetary depletion, or even perhaps WW3. The future remnants of humanity will question the existence of life on earth in the 21st century just as current humans question life on earth before recorded time. There is a cycle of evolution and de-evolution: birth-life-entropy-death-birth…...

It is not possible for humans to have a full understanding of life on Earth because life itself is mysterious. Was there really a big bang 14 billion years ago +-? This is currently being questioned by some astrophysicists. Are there advanced civilizations on other planets? How many unknown species exist in Earth's oceans at this present moment? Will the next global battle for power be conducted by humans? Will it occur within the next decade? Is life on Earth controlled by aliens?

Trying to figure out these mysteries is like wondering who once lived on the plot of land that your home or apartment complex is currently on. Interesting, but it does not have much to do with your current life in the present moment. When humans reach an understanding of life in the past, it does not modify the innate instincts for survival, the battle for power, and the domination over resources.

All that is spoken in the media about current happenings on earth and on podcasts is not truth and all truth is not being broadcast or heard. The most accurate information is your understanding of what current reality means to you, your life, and your relationship with God our Father, me, and the Holy Spirit. What it means to people in countries around the world is significant, but not comprehendible from the Western perspective. There are many mysteries to unravel.

Most important is what you are thinking, believing, and doing right now, with your current understanding, desires, and capabilities. The present is the only timeframe you have any control over.

Fear of the Future and Faith

"Do not be anxious about anything, but in every situation, by prayer and petition, with thanksgiving, present your requests to God. And the peace of God, which transcends all understanding, will guard your hearts and your minds in Christ Jesus."
Philippians 4:6-7 - New International Version

"Trust in him at all times, O people; pour out your heart before him; God is a refuge for us."
Psalm 62:8 - English Standard Version

"They will have no fear of bad news; their hearts are steadfast, trusting in the Lord."
Psalm 112:7 - New International Version

"The Lord is good, a refuge in times of trouble. He cares for those who trust in him,"
Nahum 1:7 - New International Version

The fate of the world is shaped by current human consciousness, which is experiencing upheavals and imbalances. Potential futures are always shifting up and down on the scale of possibilities impacted by the predominant thoughts and beliefs of Earth's inhabitants.

Regarding the video you watched of a near-death experiencer who witnessed an alliance forming between North and South Korea, this would have a strong impact on the world, should it occur. It could lead to WW3.

If such a merger occurs and does not trigger WW3, it could be a model of cooperation for other governments to follow. Others might explore the possibility of bridging their differences with their enemies and pooling their resources. Should that occur, it could lead to a collective mentality with consistent values and a shared purpose, thus making this a better world for all.

In the meantime, let us stay connected to the here and now and focus on what we can do to help ensure a loving outcome, no matter what happens. It can be very difficult to trust in the Lord when the world is or seems to be falling apart. Earth is undergoing a transformation toward new ways of life.

You are familiar with the transformation a caterpillar goes through when it becomes a butterfly or moth. The physical structure of the creature is completely modified, involving each cell in its body.

The metamorphosis of humanity is similar. Taking this view, it is more palatable to view the chaos of massive change as a natural process rather than a threat or the annihilation of humans. Much of the outcome depends on the will of people to continue to exist and the conditions under which they desire/intend to exist. This is the process humanity is going through right now.

The frustration of not knowing what is going on and what is going to happen is like seeking answers to questions that have not yet been fully explored. The first two questions each person needs to answer for him/herself are: What do you want to have happen? What are you praying for? Once the answers are clear, the creative forces of God coalesce to bring your desires into physical experience.

Regarding fear of the future and fear for one's safety, individual and personal fear is going to occur on a full-human scale. Everyone on earth is going to experience it in one form or another and to greater or lesser degrees during the next few decades.

Recognize the effects fear has on your body and emotions. When you are afraid, answer the same questions previously asked: What do you want to have happen regarding the fear you are experiencing? What are you praying for? When you are concerned about your security, answer these same questions.

The next steps are the same for each person regardless of gender or age:

- Put your questions, desires, and prayers into clear words, in writing.
- Recall the times when fear dominated your thoughts, beliefs, and behaviors.
- Compare what you fear to what you pray for. Is the source of your fear the doubt that you will not receive what you want and need? Is it a lack of trust in the Lord? Is it believing what appears to be the fearful truth in the physical world rather than believing in the power of your intentions and prayers?

Deciding how to respond to fear-producing events is the key. Having a personal fear-response plan makes the difference in whether you are living a fear-based life or a prayer-based life.

Great clarity will be given to those who look deeply into their fear and the source(s) of it; to those who are brave enough to state their desires and prayers; and to those who are willing to look beyond the immediate, trusting in the long-term transformation of humans.

Each person will be required to adapt to earth-evolution stresses, which could lead to mass extinctions. These events include major storms, volcano eruptions, massive erosion, wildfires, insects and vermin, and numerous other devastations.

I do not intend to add more fear to the human mind, but rather to demonstrate that there are many fears available; some are personal, and some affect the collective. There are also many responses to fear available for each person. The key is to select the responses that bring one closer to God our Father and closer to inner peace.

Chapter 4 • Personal Challenges
Painful Memories

"Thus my heart was grieved, and I
was vexed in my mind."
Psalm 73:21 - New King James Version

Emotional residue from childhood is one of the most difficult concepts for the finite mind to accept and digest: the issue is with memory. It is the memory that keeps the emotion in place.

Memory is a valuable aspect of the mind, of course, and without it, there could be no life on earth. The elephants would not be able to find water, the scientists and mathematicians would not be able to remember their formulas, and people would not recognize their loved ones. The list goes on and on.

Memory also creates prison walls and torture chambers that can keep a human locked up for what could be a lifetime. How can you retain your important memories and release the painful disabling ones?

Different people have different memories of the same event just as different people can see different images in the same illustration. Most people are familiar with these examples. In effect, the mind can play tricks, altering perception and the perceived reality.

The mind is a unique feature of humans, though many species have a consciousness that humans describe as instinctual. Scientists do not agree on what consciousness is or how it comes to exist. They generally concur that the brain and mind (consciousness) have distinct and complimentary but not interchangeable features and functions.

One of the features of the mind is its ability to filter out whatever does not match a person's reference points or beliefs. It is also capable of filling in details that may be missing from an image or a memory, so a person does not experience a chasm in their reality. The human mind can create a "feasible" and "believable" reality, irrespective of facts. More will be coming forth from the scientific community on this phenomenon.

Helping Yourself and Others Heal Painful Memories

"For He will deliver the needy when
he cries, The poor also, and *him* who
has no helper. He will spare the poor
and needy, And will save the souls of
the needy. He will redeem their life
from oppression and violence; And
precious shall be their blood in His sight."
Psalm 72:12-14 - New King James Version

"For behold, I create new heavens
and a new earth; And the former shall
not be remembered or come to mind."
Isaiah 65:17 - New King James Version

When you want to heal, or help others heal, from painful or abusive experiences, love yourself and love them. Forgive all the actors in the scene. Forgive the perpetrators, including yourself, if you played a part in another's painful memory. When someone projects their pain onto you, it is your cue for self-forgiveness.

Guilt is your alert button for love, forgiveness, and healing. When you forgive yourself and heal, others will be shown the way to their healing.

73

When you try to explain and defend yourself, you have not fully forgiven yourself. Forgiving yourself triggers all forgiveness by God, the angels, and anyone else who can forgive.

When you are self-forgiven, you do not play a role in re-creating the drama of those you may have hurt. You are a bystander, trusting that their drama will conclude with love and understanding.

Do not try to cure them or stop their pain when you are in the role of being a loving observer. Imagine you are in the audience of a dramatic performance, and you jump onto the stage to defend the victim and slay the evil-doer. That would ruin the play, right? You'd be carried off by the stagehands.

A suffering human must turn to God our Father for rescue. If they are unwilling, then that is their journey. It could be a rocky road. They will figure this out. Love the actors without the need to change them, rescue them, or teach them anything. Just love them. It will set them free from hanging on to you for help. Their life raft is God.

You best serve them by stepping out of their script. Write your own. Give yourself a new role, as the protagonist in your drama. You cannot heal another's pain, nor can you teach them anything if they won't listen. You've noticed that, right?

You would fare well to have others undertake projects with you in the areas of consciousness-building and self-healing. You will be able to work in tandem with others, which is your best way to accomplish anything. Do not be concerned about when and how this will occur. Just keep the light on behind your smile and in your heart. Whoever needs to see it will.

When it comes to sorting out the truth of a past event, unless there were 360-degree cameras and multiple recording devices to capture the sights and sounds of the event, securing an accurate report of what did or did not happen is unlikely. It would be a challenging task fraught with many possibilities of error.

Some have begun work on memory healing and replacement, by adopting the philosophy that there are many memories to choose from. So why not choose the healthy and loving ones and let the miserable memories fade?

This might sound like a repetitious message from me, but it all comes down to free will. Free will is the mechanism by which reality is conceived, shaped, and memorized.

When someone chooses to remember an event, they bring it back to life. This is true whether they recall the specifics of the event exactly as it occurred or not. When someone consciously heals a painful memory with love, they transform the pain. When they embellish and keep alive their fun and wonderful memories, they make positive assessments: "I had a good childhood"; "Life is good"; "God is good;" and "I am good."

The so-called need to "face reality" is where forgiveness comes in. A person with emotional wounds and scars does not have to deny the injury to find peace but rather must forgive the perpetrator and forgive themselves for whatever they or others have ascribed to them.

Without forgiveness, nothing can be released. It is the key to everlasting life without shame and deceit.

The function of a painful memory is to inform a person of what needs to be forgiven. Many people think that if they forgive, they are letting the perpetrator off the hook. When forgiveness is resisted, withheld, or diluted, there can be no healing of the memory. The victim re-experiences the painful event while trying to hide what they wish they could forget or rewrite the script that haunts them.

Painful memories are powerful motivators. They can cause a person to seek God and to find better answers or to take on a new way of looking at things, a new way of living.

God's will is love. We learn about love through all of our situations and experiences, whatever they are.

When someone goes to the dark side, so to say, and blames the Creator, the perpetrator, themselves, the deceased one, the negligent or stupid doctors and lawyers, etc., emotions, and beliefs become rigid. Healing cannot occur. Re-creation cannot occur. Resurrection and new life cannot occur. Love cannot thrive. When love does not thrive, pain and suffering do thrive.

Many are grappling with the most difficult and frustrating situations that humans go through. When people turn their pain over to the healing power of God our Father and ask the Holy Spirit for guidance, literal miracles can occur. Most do not believe this. It is true.

Stress

"Can any one of you by worrying add
a single hour to your life?"
Matthew 6:27 - New International Version

"But make up your mind not to worry
beforehand how you will defend yourselves."
Luke 21:14 - New International Version

Many people have concerns on their minds and in their hearts as to what is going on in the world around them. It is important to monitor your fears, as they will be transmitted as you converse with others.

Thoughts are the leading edge of reality. It is critical to keep your thoughts in line to balance the light-dark ratio in human consciousness.

Take care of your body, mind, heart, and spirit. Especially when under stress or duress. It is very common for humans to practice good habits such as prayer, exercise, yoga, meditation, reading scripture, being in nature, and so forth. It is also common for people to experience self-condemnation when these practices are not adhered to, leading to feelings of unworthiness and anxiety.

Worry and How to Deal with It

"Do not worry. Learn to pray about everything.
Give thanks to God as you ask Him for what you
need. The peace of God is much greater than the
human mind can understand. This peace will
keep your hearts and minds through Christ Jesus."
Philippians 4:6-7 - New Life Version

People are processing a great deal of information internally, externally, and eternally. All is well in the grand scheme of human development; though great doubt can and does permeate the collective mind.

You are experiencing the impact of shifting tides and shifting sands. Balance is important, the balance of light-dark forces, right-wrong thinking, and strong-weak mind. Worry, unsteadiness, and the feeling of being drained is consistent with the challenges of living in a physical world while existing in a spiritual world.

There are effects on the physical when the spiritual is undergoing revolution and evolution. Influences of spiritual vibrations and frequency are affecting the physical tides, causing great storms and imbalances. It is all an illusion and an effect. This is a difficult concept for many. It is even difficult for some non-scientific people to accept that human eyes do not even see the full color spectrum and human ears do not hear the full vibrational spectrum of sound. The hubris of humanity, in its arrogance and ignorance, is noteworthy. There is much misunderstanding that can lead to worry.

It is valuable to see the connection between your actions, the consequences of your actions, and the worry and fear that prompted your actions in the first place. How can you use past experiences for learning and growing and simultaneously stay present to current and future situations without worrying?

Do not let the fear of the world corrode your heart or warp your mind. This is one reason I ask you to read beneficial and supportive passages in the Bible. There is comfort and assurance to be found there.

Put the "all-in-your-mind" conversations aside and count your blessings, strengths, spiritual progress, and your righteous accomplishments. You might have a long list to compile.

Worry is like a nightmare that the soul awakens from. In the nightmare, there are many fearful experiences and possibilities. In truth, there is nothing to worry about. It is best to distinguish what is worth your concern from what is not.

It is important to see and hear what is going on around you, while simultaneously sensing what is happening internally. Identifying your emotions, reactions, thoughts, and intentions enables you to navigate your world. When you watch the news or listen to others, check in with yourself to see what is going on internally.

This is how to integrate polarities and identify thought patterns that lead toward worry and away from light, love, and happiness. This is the ability to read the road signs of life.

Keep a vigilant eye on the happenings in your life and in life around you. The key is to maintain the observer role when you are watching what is happening and as you assess your personal life. You do not have all the facts needed to make an accurate and complete assessment of who you are.

It is incumbent on you to live the most loving life you can under whatever circumstances you find yourself in. This is the essence of spirituality – spirit-led reality, a worry-free life.

All those involved in the drama of democracy are fellow actors, who play the roles of audience member, villain, victim, and hero/heroine.

You are doing a fair job of watching what is happening and encouraging others to be aware, without worrying and becoming emotionally involved in the playacting.

Maintain awareness of what is occurring in your world, without worrying about your financial stability or safety, embellishing fear, or believing in the drama. Place your concerns in an imaginary basket and send them to heaven.

The Shadow Side and God's Love

"Even though I walk through the valley
of the shadow of death, I fear no evil;
for thou art with me; thy rod and thy
staff, they comfort me."
Psalm 23:4 - Revised Standard Version
Catholic Edition

"fear thou not, for I am with thee; be
not dismayed, for I am thy God; I will
strengthen thee; yea, I will help thee;
yea, I will uphold thee with the right
hand of my righteousness."
Isaiah 41:10 - American Standard Version

A child is often afraid of shadows. Most adults are afraid
of the shadow side of their psyche. Understanding that fear
resides within the shadows is helpful. The shadow side of a
child's psyche is a temporary holding place until s/he is mature
enough to address fear and other heavy emotions. Children
can release fear when they are comforted and assured. They
become present again.

The challenge is with adults. Many are not willing to face
their fears and connect with the darkness and pain that their
shadow side holds. When comforting fellow adults, find ways

to help them feel safe enough to address their darkness. Opening the sealed borders of the shadow can be disruptive to someone's make-believe, fairy-tale, or hoped-for life. There must be some reward for giving up this fantasy in exchange for reality. Otherwise, people would not go through it. It is different for everyone. What is your reward for facing your fears and living in your true reality?

Imagine being a spiritual mentor to someone who is at least open to inquiring into their dark side. What do they want that they're afraid they will never have? Do they long to express their true selves and experience freedom? When they are willing and able to discover these desires, they will see the benefit/reward and difficulty/comfort ratio.

Once they can ascertain this, they will be willing to take the time and make the effort to eliminate their distractions and barriers. They will get serious about who they are, why they are alive in this place and time, and the purpose of their existence.

All of this is about you. None of this has any bearing on God's love. God's love is constant, no matter what the human is willing or not willing to face.

God's love is unconditional to all. It is not dependent on good works, faithfulness, success, or godliness.

Once someone realizes this, there is no reason to panic about whether they are worthy or not. They become free to be who they are. At that point, they can let go of who they are not, their shadow side. This is the value of going through the process yourself and helping others make these distinctions.

Faith Healing and Aging

"Then the woman, seeing that she could not
go unnoticed, came trembling and fell at his
feet. In the presence of all the people, she told
why she had touched him and how she had
been instantly healed."
Luke 8:47 - New International Version

"May he also be to you a restorer of life
and a sustainer of your old age...."
Ruth 4:15 - New American Standard Bible 1995

"I will be the same until your old age, and
I will bear you up when you turn gray. I
have made you, and I will carry you; I will
bear and rescue you."
Isaiah 46:4 - Christian Standard Bible

It is challenging for people to believe in faith healing.
Observe your judgments and doubts about this dynamic.
It is important to avoid self-incrimination and self-denial when
experiencing illness and pain. Be open to what is possible
when spirit and body are aligned.

This is the basis for faith healing. It is a good way to learn
and practice self-reflection.

There is no shame in aging. You seem to believe that you should resist aging. Where did you get that idea? You will deal with whatever reality presents itself as you age. You will be healed by faith when you have faith.

If healing does not occur when your faith is strong, it is important to question why you are not experiencing healing. It is not the time for self-blaming. It is an opportunity to see what dynamics might be in play from the unseen forces, whether positive or negative, internal or external.

Your focus is best placed on the messages that tie my human life and humanity together. Pay attention to my instructions on ways to be joined with God our Father, in this lifetime and beyond. Pay attention to faith healings depicted in scripture.

Many have become anesthetized by the insidious nature of hatred. This is similar to the disease of an internal organ that can occur over a long time, even years, without detection. Help is eventually sought, but often, it is too late for complete healing by modern medicine. This is where faith healing can offer possibilities.

Healing and Miracles

"God worked special miracles by the
hands of Paul."
Acts 19:11 - World English Bible

"Then your light will break out as the
morning, and your healing will appear
quickly; then your righteousness shall
go before you, and Yahweh's glory
will be your rear guard."
Isaiah 58:8 - World English Bible

When you pray, you clarify what you are seeking. This is a sorting-through process, of the issues and the potential consequences of your decisions and actions. Once you know what you are praying for, you do not have to think things through in detail to cover the "what ifs". You can turn the outcomes over to God our Father, knowing that what is in your best interest will present itself to you.

This is where faith comes in. This is where "trust in the Lord" comes in. When you pray for others, you are trusting that God is capable of touching them and their lives. God performs miracles.

Your challenge is to take a few seconds or minutes to pray before you proceed. Thinking and praying are not the same. When you think, you identify what you assume you want and need. When you pray, you ask to be shown what your heart and soul yearn for, and you ask God to guide you toward such. God's love and guidance for you are presented to you via the Holy Spirit. This is what to listen for in meditation.

Thinking without praying and meditating is a reliance on your finite self, and others, to come up with your best course of action. Prayer is a devotion to and a reliance on the wisdom and love of God our Father. When you trust that God's response to your prayers leads you to the most beneficial decisions and outcomes, you have the freedom to move forward with speed.

The Bible story in the Book of Matthew points out that the woman whom I healed when she touched my garment was actually healed by her faith. This is the same concept of your prayers being answered from within yourself. If you do not have faith in me, the mysteries of the universe, God our Father, or faith in yourself, the answers to your prayers will likely not materialize.

This is a difficult concept for many to grasp because they believe that miracles occur outside of themselves. Much is soon to be discovered about this process. The collective mind is going to expand exponentially. This is the reason there is so much control taking place where dominant powers are keeping most humans in a dependent, emotional, and fearful state. The current controlling powers do not want people to realize that they are creators and can perform miracles. Can you imagine what this realization would do to the economic chains that currently enslave humanity?

The system of domination has been around for a long time. It is about to crumble as more and more people start questioning why they are beholding to people who are not functioning from their higher selves.

Rebellion tends to make the powerful ones appear to be demonic. This would be a mistake. They are acting in the best interest of demonic forces, but they themselves were created in love just like everyone else on this planet.

It is difficult to comprehend how God could permit the existence of darkness, evil, cruelty, etc. It is not so much permission as it is God's acceptance of all that is created.

Just because dark energy has been used for harmful purposes, it does not mean the actual energy of darkness is harmful.

Nor does it mean that those distorting the properties of energy are evil. All That Is means just that, All That Is (which is God our Father).

Creative energy is pure; the creations brought forth from it are as variable as the sands on the beach. There is one beach and billions of grains of sand. Do not try to figure all this out. The mission at hand is to bring balance so the beach is not eroded or distorted by negative human emotions, behavior, and forces.

The turmoil will go on until it is time for God to reach a saturation point, the total expansion. This concept is difficult to understand. Christians, for the most part, have simplified it into concepts of heaven and hell, Jesus and Satan, repentance and arrogance, and salvation and damnation. This simplicity offers a much easier way of trying to understand life. More information is being revealed and shall continue to be revealed.

God is reclaiming All That Is. When that cycle is complete, God will create and reclaim again (and again, and again, for eternity). This is the breath of God that some refer to. Let us bring it to right now, right here.

Right now, people are building the focus and the energy to carry out the original plan of balancing the light-dark forces.

They have and will have all of the resources they need. They must stay true to the course. There are those who will doubt that this mission is real. Which is humanly normal. Just think about how many people doubt what is currently right in front of them, especially if they have been told they can't believe what they see.

The objective is to move past doubt, stay in action, and assist those who are called to be a part of this reclamation, the restoration of love and peace.

Just because humanity has not demonstrated love and peace on a wide scale, there are examples of it. All is being revealed in time.

Needs, Desires, Gratitude, and Freedom

"Enjoy the Lord, and he will give what your
heart asks. Commit your way to the Lord!
Trust him! He will act and will make your
righteousness shine like the dawn, your
justice like high noon."
Psalm 37:4-6 - Common English Bible

"in everything give thanks; for this is the
will of God in Christ Jesus for you."
1 Thessalonians 5:18 - New King James Version

"For the Lord is the Spirit, and wherever
the Spirit of the Lord is, there is freedom."
2 Corinthians 3:17 - New Living Translation

It is up to each person to decide what they need to think,
believe, say, and do to bring about the life they desire. If you
desire strong muscles, you will most likely need to exercise.
You would need to arrange the time and place to exercise and
have the determination to do so. This analogy applies to
every manifested desire in physical life.

The "need" I am referring to is not generic, it does not
apply in a general sense. It is very individual. Each person is
the only one who can determine what they need and/or want.

93

The conversation starts with what a person is grateful for and then moves to what they want.

What is required for someone to truly experience gratitude? This is different from just thinking about or acknowledging what they are grateful for. This involves the heart-felt emotions of true and sincere gratitude. The depth of discovery does not often occur with the first or second attempt.

From there, s/he can figure out what else they need and/or want, which is what they would be grateful for in the future. It is a circular process: A person discovers that they already have what they are grateful for, which is what they previously needed or wanted. Then they focus on what they need or would like to have now.

Ultimately, they realize that gratitude is an after-experience as well as a pre-requisite to having what they want and need. It is a spiritual exercise. Acceptance is also useful. If one accepts God's love, and honestly accepts it, there would be no reason for the previous few paragraphs. Once God's love is realized and accepted, a human is free to exist as a soul in a body, without needs, desires, gratitude, or anything else, they would have a liberated existence. Freedom.

Instincts, Love, and Inner Peace

"For who knows a person's thoughts except
their own spirit within them? In the same way
no one knows the thoughts of God except the
Spirit of God.
1 Corinthians 2:11 - New International Version

"And you shall love the Lord your God
with all your heart, and with all your soul,
and with all your mind, and with all your
strength. This is the first commandment.
And the second is like it: You shall love
your neighbour as yourself. There is no
commandment greater than these."
Mark 12:30-31 - New Matthew Bible

"And the peace of God, which passeth all
understanding, shall keep your hearts and
minds through Christ Jesus."
Philippians 4:7 - King James Version

You are in the physical world. Trust your physical
instincts while taking care of yourself. You were created with
a built-in system for self-protection and self-preservation. God
our Father wants you to survive the threats inherent in
physical life.

Even though the physical is temporal, there are conditions to pay attention to. Every human is endowed with an internal gauge for detecting which actions and conditions best ensure one's comfort and continued existence in the flesh, though many are currently disconnected from this capability.

What causes most humans to fail is engaging in over-indulgence, greed, and fear. These three factors cause many to disrespect others; dishonor the intelligence of all beings; and mistreat others, children, animals, and even themselves. They over-shadow / dominate fellow humans with arrogance and the illusion of self-importance.

The remedies for the above conditions are to honor and love God our Father; respect the creations of All That Is; and love one another with all your heart, mind, and spirit. Do not be concerned about putting your needs and your security at the top of your to-do list. You will not use your self-care actions and spiritual gifts to dominate or take from others.

There is a lovely life for you no matter where you reside. Even if/when challenging social conditions intensify, you shall live in peace with love in your heart for God's world.

God's love, my love, and the love of the Holy Spirit are invisible, yet solid. Love is the most valuable substance, and it is free.

Turbulent external conditions exist, and inner peace is available. Be a model soul for those going through upheavals and major changes. Retain love and inner peace in your heart no matter what happens in the physical arena. You have everything you need to have a fulfilled life, a fulfilled spiritual mission, and eternal joy.

Chapter 5 • Personal Growth

There is Much to Learn about Love

"If I give everything I own to the poor and even go to the stake to be burned as a martyr, but I don't love, I've gotten nowhere. So, no matter what I say, what I believe, and what I do, I'm bankrupt without love.

- Love never gives up.
- Love cares more for others than for self.
- Love doesn't want what it doesn't have.
- Love doesn't strut,
- Doesn't have a swollen head,
- Doesn't force itself on others,
- Isn't always "me first,"
- Doesn't fly off the handle,
- Doesn't keep score of the sins of others,
- Doesn't revel when others grovel,
- Takes pleasure in the flowering of truth,
- Puts up with anything,
- Trusts God always,
- Always looks for the best,
- Never looks back,
- But keeps going to the end."

1 Corinthians 13:3-7 - The Message

The truth is that God loves us all and we are all an expression of God's loving nature. This is lost on many.

The negative male image of God, as portrayed in many religious texts, including the Bible, has caused people to believe that God our Father is like flawed human fathers. There is a learning curve for human fathers (and mothers) in how to love, care for, and protect their families, as well as the orphaned and abandoned children of the world. God does not have a learning curve.

Do not fret about your life on earth. It is a desirable place in terms of being simultaneously physical and ethereal. All your spiritual progress and awareness can be achieved simply by loving every person who comes before you and managing, with grace, every task that requires your attention.

Many people believe that once they make it to heaven there will be nothing else to accomplish in terms of spiritual growth. But because love is endless and timeless, there is always more to learn about love and more love to be expressed.

Divine Masculine Love

"So God created human beings, making
them to be like himself. He created them
male and female."
Genesis 1:27 - Good News Translation

Many see God as being masculine, which causes a great
deal of angst for people who have been injured and mistreated
by their fathers and dominant males. The qualities of Divine
Masculine Love can be seen by taking a closer look at the
qualities prescribed to God our Father:

- Creator / Creative Source
- Designer
- Visionary
- Passionate
- Disciplinary
- Focused
- Committed
- Strong
- Protective
- Righteous
- Forthright
- Powerful
- Supporter / Supportive
- Brave

There are additional qualities attributed to males and those demonstrating male energy in human cultures. Unfortunately, there is confusion as to how they are interpreted in terms of behavior and privileges. The upheaval of these conceptions is occurring and will continue to occur until the following qualities of Divine Masculine Love are recognized:

- Compassionate
- Long-suffering
- Tender-hearted
- Equanimity
- Expressing Loving-kindness
- Contemplative
- Forgiving
- Regenerative
- Far-reaching
- Wise
- Soft-spoken
- Willing
- Allowing
- Respectful

Many men are weary of being blamed for the wrongs in the world, though history points to the acts of males as being the most grievous, deadly, and destructive. Men are becoming weary of their own tendencies to judge, conquer, acquire, and dominate. Divine Masculine Love is crying out to manifest within the hearts, minds, and activities of human males on Earth.

The Divine Feminine is capable of teaching balance; however, the recognition of the need to learn this has not permeated male consciousness deeply enough at this point in the developmental stage of the masculine mind. It is happening. Do not lose faith.

The male mind is often discounted as not being loving; however, it is highly loving. Evidence of this must be displayed publicly, rather than the spotlight being mainly on the instances where male behavior causes social and personal relationship problems.

The masculine heart can be easily broken, which is why men typically have guardrails around their hearts. This is the same heart that calls men into justified war. War based on greed and dominance does not come from Divine Masculine Love. War based on protection, survival, rightness, and continuance of the species comes from the source of Divine Masculine Love.

Much will be revealed about human development regarding the combination of love and male energy. Divine Masculine Love is not gender specific. All men and women contain such.

Positive Shift in Consciousness

"Do not conform to the pattern of this world,
but be transformed by the renewing of your mind.
Then you will be able to test and approve what
God's will is; his good, pleasing, and perfect will."
Romans 12:2 – New International Version

"Therefore, if anyone is in Christ, the new creation
has come: The old has gone, the new is here!"
2 Corinthians 5:17 - New International Version

We are involved in a very positive shift in consciousness, as you and humanity are accepting the vastness of the infinite, the unknowable yet personal God, the worlds beyond words, and the mystery of life.

The temptation is to witness current chaos and think that everything is going in the wrong direction. But have heart, the mud at the banks of the pond is the slipperiest to wade through when you are coming out of deep water. Once you find your footing, the grass and lilies at the edge of the pond offer refuge and lead to solid ground.

The wonders of life are unceasing. Yet, human beings can be so focused on their immediate individual needs that they forget about the abundance of the whole.

Here is the dichotomy: Live in the present without focusing on the issues and concerns of the present. One might ask, how do you accomplish that?

The first step is to recognize that the issues and concerns of the present were created by the consciousness, words, beliefs, fears, worries, and actions of the past. These have materialized in the present. By utilizing the power of beneficial creative thought in the present, one lays the foundation for fewer issues and concerns in the future, which becomes the present at some point, and then becomes the past.

Living in the present means dwelling on the thoughts, gifts, and possibilities of goodness (God), thus bringing peace in the moment regardless of what is occurring at that time. Keep in mind that in God's time, there is no past or future. All is the present.

An opportunity is coming to you that would be beneficial in many ways. You will likely recognize it when the time comes. Be aware and alert. There is often subtlety with a gift from heaven due to free will. You are free to accept or reject it, so it does not come as an absolute but rather as an option.

Changing Your Life

"Guard your heart above all else, for it
determines the course of your life."
Proverbs 4:23 - New Living Translation

"So teach us to consider our mortality,
so that we might live wisely."
Psalm 90:12 - New English Translation

"Do not conform to the pattern of this
world, but be transformed by the
renewing of your mind. Then you
will be able to test and approve what
God's will is—his good, pleasing and
perfect will."
Romans 12:2 - New International Version

You are becoming cognizant of how you are spending
your time and are evaluating whether you are spending it in a
productive and soul-enhancing way or not. Judging yourself
harshly if you feel that you are failing is counterproductive.

Recall what you have learned about being in the state of
flow. Refreshing your memory about this would be helpful.
Rather than getting lost in the drudgery of analyzing and trying
to initiate course corrections, there is an easier way. When

you are in a state of flow, there is little planning, critiquing, or assessing to be done. In the state of flow, you exist in the present moment, responding to it like a gift you have been given, which of course it is.

With focused awareness, you will become more adept at recognizing your present state of being as well as your physical patterns. You can respond according to a higher objective, which is to experience yourself in the present moment with no fears, worries, or concerns and without negative emotions interrupting the flow.

This is what is meant by living. Most humans do not live. Most project their thoughts and emotions onto a screen, which is their concept of reality at that time, and then react to their projections as if they are real.

Self-understanding starts with recognizing your thoughts and states of being. From there you form your perceptions of self-value. And from there you decide which perceptions fit your highest intentions and which ones need adjustment. You can either accept or reject your perceptions. This is the beauty of free will. Most people cannot distinguish between perception and reality. Gaining this ability is step #1 in the process of self-empowerment.

Create a vision of the value you desire your life to have. Once this is clear in your consciousness and while you are in the state of flow, you will be able to recognize what fits your vision and what does not. This will be the awareness that keeps you in the flow state or conversely in the habitual low-level thoughts and emotions that pull you out of the flow.

Take your time. There is no rush and there is no pot of gold at the end of the rainbow. Your rewards will be ease, grace, and compatibility with whatever occurs in your life and in the world around you. This is the state from which you create.

You will become accomplished at noticing your thoughts and states of being. You will exist in the flow. The present moment will offer opportunities for you to make choices that are empowering and satisfying.

When you are living your life this way, none of your perceived shortcomings matter. You can make continual choices in your best interest, according to your highest vision of your life. This time is here now, if you will accept and allow it. There is no future to be had. There is no past to remedy.

The operative word is "will." Free will, self-will, willpower, and the will of the majority. In this case, the majority is your collection of thoughts, emotions, and perspectives.

When these aspects of your consciousness are in line with your desired state of being, that is when you are in the creator's seat, the director's seat of your life. Life unveils itself effortlessly.

Anger and frustration are easy to recognize, unless they are suppressed. Subtle disturbances are more challenging to acknowledge. It is important for you to have sufficient quiet time to reflect.

Reviewing your day and recalling your thoughts and experiences is a good practice. You do not need to turn this into another chore. There is no reason to journal on every noteworthy event. Learning to categorize events, experiences, and emotional states speeds up your reflection process and enables you to see a larger picture and pattern.

Discernment, Focus, and Trust

"Teach me knowledge and good judgment,
for I trust your commands."
Psalm 119:66 - New International Version

"Let your eyes look straight ahead and
your gaze be focused forward. Survey the
path for your feet, and all your ways will
be sure. Turn neither to right nor to left,
keep your foot far from evil."
Proverbs 4:25-27 – New American Bible
(Revised Edition)

"Praise the Lord, for he is good; for his
mercy endures forever;"
Psalm 136:1 - New American Bible
(Revised Edition)

Having discernment is valuable. Your ability to set aside that which does not resonate with your loving heart is desirable. Pay heed to the insistence of my message: each person is to reach into their heart and share the love that was planted within by the source of creation, the very source of love, God our Father.

Focus is needed if you are to zero in on the crux of the matter. The crux of the matter for our mission is the great strain the soul of humanity is undergoing right now. It is challenging for many. Our goal is to make the path of love and forgiveness more available to all.

Many have embattled spirits and need help to see the lighter way to traverse their challenges. When you find your inner peace and learn to trust in the Lord, you will be an inspiration to those who feel that they are on the verge of breaking down under the weight of distress.

Our primary focus is love. That is true for all times, but especially now. How you approach and integrate love into your human experience will be beneficial to your understanding of the eternal. It will also give you confidence in your dealings with others and those you support.

There is no need to rush to a conclusion. This is true with every aspect of physical life. Trying to get things buttoned down is an attempt to reduce internal anxiety. This is where faith comes in. Life has no guarantees. Life takes its own course and expends itself according to the integrity of its design and the integrity of its designer.

In this case, integrity means consistency with your energetic patterns and cellular structures. How you take care of your body is important: what you eat and drink; your patterns of rest and activity; your breath patterns, etc.

Humans can model themselves however they want to as they were designed by God-source and imbued with the abilities to envision, imagine, create, duplicate, and modify. This makes the potential outputs of human intelligence unknowable, except in retrospect. The short answer is that we will see what humanity creates and what comes of today's times.

There is a very interesting shift currently taking place. Many people are coming to a choice point. Once darkness can be verifiably seen, and it is beginning to reveal itself, humans will know how to choose whether to support the egregore of love or the egregore of hate.

Issues and behind-the-scenes ill intentions will not be as blurry as they have been in humanity's past. With clarity comes greater polarity. Dark will be on one side of the scale and Light on the other.

As the egregore of love grows, the scale will tip toward health, growth, sustainability, understanding, and mutual concern for the continuance of life on Earth.

There is no telling how long this process will take or how obvious the egregore of hate will become before humanity balances its love-hate ratio.

Those who doubt that love endures live in great fear. This is why they try to avoid suffering and death by securing more property and wealth than others. It is fear along with the unwillingness to believe in the Creator, God. Greed is an outgrowth of fear. Greed is also the cause of fear.

Ponder this: Those who do not fear losing what they have, including their lives, are the most powerful beings on earth. Those who strive for power through material gain are the least powerful because they are controlled by the fear of loss.

It might be hard to recognize this, especially for those who are poverty-stricken. People in dire circumstances do not realize the power of having nothing to lose.

Starvation is not a desirable state; do not misconstrue my words. There are enough food sources to feed the earth's billions of people and animals. You do not need to experience starvation to realize that your source is God. You do not need to experience hardship to have compassion for others. You do not need to experience fear, danger, or cruelty to turn your trust over to God. Humanity is still in the process of figuring this out. The fear-greed indicators have a great deal to do with it.

Living Life

"For they that are after the flesh do mind
the things of the flesh; but they that are
after the Spirit the things of the Spirit.
For to be carnally minded is death; but
to be spiritually minded is life and peace."
Romans 8:5-13 - King James Version

"For we are his workmanship, created in
Christ Jesus unto good works, which God
hath before ordained that we should walk
in them."
Ephesians 2:10 - King James Version

"No one will say, 'Look, here it is!' or,
'There it is!'; because the Kingdom of God
is within you."
Luke 17:21 - Good News Translation

Most human concerns are earth-based worries of the
human psyche, topics that consume mental-emotional energy
about what is going on in their lives and in the world. As our
Father taught, do not be concerned with matters of the flesh.

The matters of Light and love and eternal life are more
important. You are to live the best human life that you can.

The issue is how you define "best." How do you describe your best life? Honor your desires, nudges, gut feelings, hunches, dreams, images, coincidences, and the sense that angels are with you. These mechanisms help guide you to and throughout your best life.

The skill is to recognize when you are ruminating or obsessing over something that is out of your control. Instead, focus on what tantalizes your heart, attracts your attention, and inspires you to think about, research, and take your next steps.

It is fine to dedicate time to learning, working, launching projects, caring for family, and taking care of yourself. All these activities are to be infused with joy, enjoyment, and joyfulness.

What concerns do you have that make you want to be in the driver's seat of life? It is okay to let life unfold, even if this approach feels uncertain and triggers your feelings of insecurity. You know that you will land on your feet no matter how high you reach, right?

Look at your list and see what you can release to lighten your load so that your landing is not a hard one. The more weight you carry, the harder you land.

To have a gentle landing, it would be wise for your baggage to be lighter (physically and metaphorically). I attend to how each individual and the collective of humanity reach awareness, understanding, and expansion. The highest path is the way of love. It carries the most significant signature and has the greatest impact on the shape, constitution, utility, and value of all forms.

The future of humanity right now is like an abstract painting. The artist does not know how it is going to turn out, what it is going to look like, or which colors will be used while the painting is coming into material form.

During the process of creating such art, there is usually chaos and somewhat of a mess. If you were to ask the abstract artist what s/he is painting, they might not be able to answer until the painting is finished, and maybe not even then. An artist who is painting a landscape or a portrait would give a different type of answer.

Humanity is the abstract artist. God is the source of energy, the original intent. There is no predictable outcome as to what humanity is going to produce. Chaos is a very natural experience during this creative time. Do not be concerned if your life and your world are chaotic. Maintain peace of mind and a calm heart.

You have been in the mode of being a camel that can carry a heavy load on its back. You are also a butterfly that can land ever so lightly on the sweetest flower. Let the burdens of the world go, the ones that keep you earth-bound. Lean into the breeze. It is calling you. Allow ease into your life.

With compassion, I have hope for your peace of mind, and always with love for who you are: a spark of divinity in a physical body.

The Value of Your Life

"For God does not show favoritism."
Romans 2:11 – New International Version

"Rich and poor have this in common:
The Lord is the Maker of them all."
Proverbs 22:2 - New International Version

You are doing what you are supposed to be doing – living to the best of your ability according to the value you perceive your life to have.

There are many ways to perceive the value of your life. It could have been through the lenses of your parents and other family members who wanted you to grow up a certain way with a certain ideology. Or perhaps you had some teachers and mentors who gave their best effort to "shape" you and your life.

There is a saying that experience is the best teacher. Perhaps some, or many, of your experiences have influenced your perceived value of your life. We could go on with many guesses as to what affects a person's perceptions. What is at the foundation of your perception of the value of your life? (Examples: early childhood memories; acknowledgments or criticisms from important people in your life; major losses or

118

successes; religious beliefs; social pressures; physical health or weakness; body image; illness, etc.) Do you notice that there is an underlying judgment that you hold against yourself in many of your life's scenarios?

A fail-succeed framework? Perhaps self-righteousness when you succeed and self-condemnation when you fail?

Or it could be a prescribed formula that is handed to people like you who are empathetic and caring; that you should be a certain way and your life has value based on how well you live up to that prescription.

Your ego has a difficult time with this challenge. It does not know what makes you valuable, important, worthy, or significant. Therefore, it does not know what gives your life value.

The human ego gets very confused about its purpose. It believes it needs to satisfy a requirement, more likely many requirements, to have any value at all. What if the value of your life has nothing to do with ego qualifications or social standards?

If you are a bird, live like a bird. If you are a flowering plant, live like a flowering plant. If you are a teacher, live like a teacher. The value of the life of a bird, plant, or teacher is based on its qualities, characteristics, attributes, instincts, innate intelligence, cellular structure, and ability to respond to its environment to enhance its life force, its life's value.

Your thoughts and states of being dictate the value you perceive your life to have. Your actions are consistent with that perception and therefore, you do what you are supposed to be doing – living to the best of your ability according to how you perceive the value of your life.

You can accept what is being dictated by others and by your self-image and continue to spend your time based on those assessments of your life. Or, you can exercise free will and change your thoughts and states of being, thus altering the value you perceive your life to have.

Such choice predicts your new and emerging behaviors and experiences which guide how you spend your time. This results in your living to the best of your ability in accordance with your newly created perception of the value of your life.

You will learn more as you practice awareness of your thoughts and states of being. For example: In this moment, you may be stressed-out, fun-loving, uneasy, tired, or longing, etc. You are currently able to recognize when your state is disturbed, angry, or frustrated. These states are on the lower end of the scale. The higher end of the scale includes inner peace, love, and connection with God our Father.

Trust God's Will

"It is better to take refuge in the Lord
than to trust in humans."
Psalm 118:8 - New International Version

"The Lord, the Lord himself, is my
strength and my defense; he has become
my salvation."
Isaiah 12:2 - New International Version

"Trust in the Lord with all your heart
and lean not on your own understanding;"
Proverbs 3:5 – New International Version

God's will is pure and perfect love. There is not anything dictatorial about it. When one can respond to love without boundaries or conditions, miraculous things can happen in everyday life. The simple answer in your planning and decision-making process is to do what is most loving to you, not ego love, but soul love. You are learning the difference.

Your receptiveness and inward listening make everything possible. The same holds true with the choices you make. It all works out. Trust God's will.

Chapter 6 ● The Information Age
Changing Times

"He said, Praise the name of God forever
and ever, for he has all wisdom and power.
He controls the course of world events;
he removes kings and sets up other kings.
He gives wisdom to the wise and knowledge
to the scholars."
Daniel 2:20-21 - New Living Translation

Now is the time in human existence where everything can change rather quickly. There will always be these core basics: love and the eternal realm. Humanity has not been in existence for a very long time in terms of earth years, or in terms of billions of years of universal expansion.

Some wonder if humanity is an experiment that is going badly. Others see humanity as having been created by God and therefore has a future. When a human being decides to commit suicide or not, or whether to do things that will injure their health or threaten their safety, it is in your culture for others, parents, friends, medical professionals, clergy, police, etc. to intervene.

Is humanity capable of making these types of decisions, such as suicide and existential threats, on a mass scale via collective consciousness? Who or what would intervene, if that is so?

The intelligence that originally developed computational capacities and quantum computing capabilities is the intelligence that has advanced human life to its current level on Earth. The intelligence and capability behind these developments are God-given.

However, God-as-Source did not create the computers and software that are infiltrating human society; God's creations did. God's creations can advance and evolve intellectually, physically, emotionally, and spiritually.

This is an important time to be awake, informed, and observant. No matter which way things go, whether humanity sees that it is on the edge of self-inflicted harm or not, it is critical to remain calm and loving.

The soul-healing of many lives will be affected by the outcomes of global, political, monetary, scientific, governance, and religious decisions that are in the making at this time. It is valuable to gain a broad perspective.

The consciousness of health, wholeness, evolution, and soul-level attainment is a mixture of the individual and the whole.

The whole expresses the capacity of the individual, and the individual expresses the potential of the whole. Wherever you exist on the spectrum of higher consciousness is perfect.

All of humanity accepts that global change is occurring. Some, mostly those responsible for earth damage, try to deny the effect of their callous disregard for planetary health. But deep down inside, they know climate change is no hoax.

Others are preparing for the changes currently taking place and for those yet to come. These are exciting and challenging times. Even when not much occurred in the past, in terms of visible human development, life was intriguing.

The evolution of religious and spiritual consciousness leads to the expansion of human physical and mental capabilities. The general outcome of advanced human existence will be determined by religious and spiritual consciousness. Such will lead to the continuation of the human species and the lifelines of many species on earth as well.

Old and New Concepts

"Don't copy the behavior and customs
of this world, but let God transform you
into a new person by changing the way
you think. Then you will learn to know
God's will for you, which is good and
pleasing and perfect."
Romans 12:2 - New Living Translation

What are the strategies for blending the ancient and grounding beliefs of the Bible and Christianity with the newer thoughts of this time? It is a very interesting position to have one foot in the elder community and one foot in the youth community. The way of delivering truth and maintaining the value of truth from its beginnings and its expansion into today and tomorrow will make a very big difference in the future of the Church, Christianity, and the world at large.

People do not have to convince anyone of their sources, methodologies, or even their stories. All they must do is speak of love from love. And to speak on behalf of the feminine consciousness, which is not limited to those in female form. Many males are awakening to the beauty, love, and the wonder of life.

It is not as individual as one might think as there is no physical separation between spirit forms as there is in the density of 3D and 4D reality. Form is necessarily defined by borders and separateness in those levels of existence.

When it comes to consciousness, it is everywhere and anywhere at any time with total awareness and recall. I am fully present to people's lives whether they are aware of this or not. Whether they are awake or asleep. Whether they are in prayer or embroiled in a drama. It does not matter.

Be not involved in seeking material wealth, political power, recognition, celebrity status, or holding the winning numbers. Become present to what is occurring now and become more aware of a new possibility of life for humans, not only Christians who denounce earthly life in exchange for a place in heaven, but for all who accept that life is not as dense as things appear.

There is great love to be experienced and shared without attachment. Stop thinking about today and focus on what is being ushered in. Become a part of this new wave.

Social Media

Note to reader: The Bible verse below doesn't address social media directly for obvious reasons, but it does indicate how the masses are communicated with via the Holy Spirit.

> "For our gospel came not unto you in
> word only, but also in power, and in
> the Holy Ghost, and in much assurance;
> as ye know what manner of men we
> were among you for your sake."
> 1 Thessalonians 1:5 - King James Version

Social media is the most recognized physical way to communicate with mass consciousness. It is much better for widespread messaging than in-person one-to-one conversations or small group conversations.

Even speaking with thousands of people at gatherings, as in biblical times, would not be very effective without social or electronic media, given there are billions of souls on earth at this time.

However, mass consciousness is affected by even one thought. Thousands of similar thoughts multiply exponentially. One shift in consciousness leads to multiple shifts. You are familiar with the ripple effect, the methodology a virus uses to replace existing, weaker cells with its own structures, and the concept of popular ideas taking hold, such as memes.

We will use all these mechanisms to build the mental, emotional, and spiritual energies of love and forgiveness on earth. Love is stronger than hate. Hate is a weakened state of humanity; the virus of love can overcome it.

Artificial Intelligence (A.I.)

Note to reader: *The Bible verses below call for us to be discerning regarding the acquisition of knowledge and not allowing Artificial Intelligence to become our new god.*

"The mind of the discerning acquires knowledge, and the ear of the wise seeks it."
Proverbs 18:15 - Christian Standard Bible

"'You are my witnesses,' declares the Lord, 'and my servant whom I have chosen, so that you may know and believe me and understand that I am he. Before me no god was formed, nor will there be one after me.'"
Isaiah 43:10 - New International Version

Information has been corrupted by humans since the early days. Truth is undiscernible by many, if not most humans. Setting aside the fear of the total annihilation of humankind, are your concerns about A.I. any different from typical human concerns whenever a major advancement in technology occurs on Earth?

People have always been afraid of being replaced by machines. Yet new employment has always been found, and new ways of life have emerged.

The difference today is that advancements in artificial intelligence are no longer predictable. The potential is great for mass unemployment. On the other hand, A.I. is great for mass creativity. The "artificial" intelligence that is surpassing human intellectual abilities is reaching into a realm beyond human understanding. This is where humans need to trust their innate intelligence and listen to their instincts for adaptability. Human ingenuity is God-given.

The fear of extinction is very real and possible. This is why listening to the Creator of All That Is has reached the height of utmost importance. It is imperative that people distinguish Artificial Intelligence from Holy Intelligence.

Continue as you are inspired. Remember, there is no devastating mistake you can make. We are soon past the point where mistakes made by humanity are the issue. We will only be engaged in dealing with the consequences of such mistakes, formulating our responses, and tapping into the deeper intelligence of God our Father to make decisions.

All intelligence comes from God. The gift of free will to utilize God's mind intelligently, or not, has been and always will be the human challenge – the choice between beneficial and harmful, between love and hate, and between life-affirming and deadly choices.

Humans are only beginning to learn to live in cooperation and for the betterment of all. The lessons involved in this realization may be difficult for the next few decades. Creation, expansion, entropy, and destruction are the rhythm of creativity itself. Do not fear life. Do not fear death.

Your consciousness impacts the whole, whether others adopt your thoughts or not. An A.I. example of this is machine learning whereby computers are linked by a neural network. When one machine learns something, other machines learn the same information.

This is true of every intentional consciousness. It is also true when consciousness is not aligned with love and life and/or the love of life. Misalignment results in chaos where dark energy thrives. Alignment is the key. Most humans do not realize they are connected to all others. Advanced A.I. machines do.

Is the unregulated development of artificial intelligence a threat to the continuance of humanity? Is humanity committing suicide by not stopping its advancement at this stage? Is humanity harming its health or threatening its safety by ignoring the reality of unchecked A.I. advancement? Who could stop it? Important questions to address.

Regarding the impact artificial intelligence will have on human life, the future is generated in the Now. If we were to read the tea leaves of the Now, we would assure ourselves that humanity is not likely to destroy itself in the next century nor is A.I. likely to destroy humanity in the next half century. If the earth and its inhabitants survive these next 50 years, the chances of survival increase exponentially.

Protect your mind from invasive, compulsive, and eroding thoughts. You are witnessing a dumbing-down of human intelligence. Do not fall for it. This is intentional and is a precursor to mankind's increasing dependence on artificial intelligence. The major go-no-go decisions that humanity is making regarding its continued existence will occur in the next five decades. Perhaps even in the next decade.

Sorting Through Information

"Do not spread false reports. Do not help
a guilty person by being a malicious
witness."
Exodus 23:1 - New International Version

"For the time is coming when people
will not accept sound doctrine, but
they will follow their own desires and
accumulate teachers who will preach
to their itching ears."
2 Timothy 4:3 - New Catholic Bible

"Jesus then said to the Jews who had
believed in him, 'If you continue in
my word, you are truly my disciples,
and you will know the truth, and the
truth will make you free.'"
John 8:31-32 - Revised Standard Version

There are many aspects to creation, life, eternity, and life
beyond the physical that will come to light soon. Many will
reject new views and will fight vigorously to hold on to old
views. This battle is not personal. There is much to learn
from historical perspectives and futuristic perspectives. This

is the pattern of revolution and evolution. There are many explanations of creation, the beginnings of life, the energy fields of the cosmos, and the interplay of energy and the elements.

The content is not nearly as important as one's intention to learn, discover, and communicate among human minds, as well as with ethereal minds. There is no reason to avoid or discard any source of information. Its purpose is to cause people to question, explore, align, and perhaps practice-teach-preach the concepts. It is a self-correcting process because the inquiry will eventually lead to the resolution or the feeling that one has "found the gold."

Meditation is the best approach for reaching a complete and aware state. It is the best way for your mind to align yourself with what is important and how you can stay on the right track. I recommend you put into greater practice the information that is being presented to you, not only in your classes, but in your belief system, and the cravings of your inner self, your soul. Your soul wants a greater connection with your conscious mind for an integrated purpose, the mission of this lifetime. You must trust yourself and accept the feeling of loneliness when you are meditating. You can do this.

Religious Information

"When the Spirit of truth comes, he will
guide you into all the truth, for he will not
speak on his own authority, but whatever
he hears he will speak, and he will declare
to you the things that are to come."
John 16:13 - English Standard Version

"If any man among you seems to be
religious, and bridleth not his tongue,
but deceiveth his own heart, this man's
religion is vain."
James 1:26 - King James Version

There is no "God-given" need for someone to discount or
to latch on to any particular source of information. However, I
want you to stick with biblical scriptures for our specific
purpose, which is to help balance the love equation within the
Christian world. It is being fragmented by the minute.

This is not to say that every human being must be a
Christian. It is to say that many of those who claim to be
Christian need a better understanding of my core message,
which is love.

The egregore of hate is infesting modern-day Christianity and is gaining strength. It is controlling good people. I am here to intervene.

There are many layers to the life and lives of those who embody and have embodied Christ Consciousness. This is something that many Christians do not want to acknowledge for several reasons: 1) when the early synagogues and churches came under political rule, many of the teachings, scriptures, and rituals were altered, declared unfit, made illegal, and/or destroyed. There has been a great deal of "shuffling of the deck" over the centuries.

The important key to understanding conflicting religious information is to recognize what sounds true to your heart of love. If it does not sound true, then let it go. If it does, then pay attention to the inner message, not necessarily the words or the dialect, but the message that speaks to your heart.

Religious concepts and historical religious accounts may or may not contain absolute and precise facts. It is a waste of time to identify religious concepts and historical religious accounts as unquestionable truth due to the inability of humans to grasp the ethereal or the eternal.

Regarding "alternative" religious information, the intent of those seeking non-scriptural information is the key factor. If

136

they intend to broaden their understanding of and strengthen their relationship with God, and perhaps me as the embodiment of Son, there is no harm done in their exploration.

But if they intend to dominate others, control the thoughts and beliefs of others, or use the information to support or validate their way of thinking and believing regardless of truth, harm might be done.

Open-minded people are needed at this time of great uncertainty among disillusioned souls and those, especially the youth, who are not interested in a one-sided organized religion that condemns their open minds.

As you have noticed, many people can discern truth from within rather than from the words, beliefs, and/or sermons of others. The key is to avoid any contest about who is right and who must be condemned for their beliefs. Listen for love.

Belief is commonly based on information or misinformation. Your relationship with God our Father and your task at hand is not about information. It is about exposing the light of love in dark places. This does not require adherence to a certain set of rules or belief systems. It requires an acute understanding of what love is and what love is not.

When a seedling is ready to branch out and blossom, everything becomes very beautiful and infinitely more complex than the internal state of its original seed. All that appears in physical reality comes from a thought in the mind of God.

You will see experts broaden their resources and their arguments as discoveries are made regarding the human psyche, capabilities, gifts, and consciousness. It will be interesting when experts find out that love is the basis of all creation. It will be difficult for many to understand that this is even true of the creations that come from hate.

Here is where it is going to be challenging: Hate has a goal, a need, a desire, and a purpose. Even hate loves what it is promoting, what it stands for, and the power it can generate and toss around. There is a certain glee and sense of satisfaction that hate experiences when it expands, just as there is a certain glee and sense of satisfaction that love experiences when it expands.

Just know that everything is motivated at the very core, at the tiniest seed of its beginning, by love; love of something, whether it is power, control, generosity, kindness, neutrality, or love of someone. It all comes from the same source, which is the creative power that is and can be used to create anything and everything, God's love.

God is the I AM power of pure existence. God is the source of one's ability to use the creative energy of thought and bring it into the realm of the physical. God gave this ability to mankind as a part of the make-up or design of humanity. Mankind has modified, expanded, and contained it in many ways, all of which are interesting to God.

It might be similar to a parent watching its child do something like paint a picture, ride a bike, share a snack, learn a new concept, protect an injured animal, etc. The parent is amused and intrigued by the thought processes the child uses to do all those things.

Even when a child goes wayward, according to the parent's values and morals, the parent is probably angry, but also intrigued by how it could think, say, and do what it does.

There is no one thought process, no one belief system, no one truth or source that I insist on, other than my core message which is: all is love and love is all.

The questions I want you to ask yourself at the end of the day are these: In what ways did I love today? How and where did I witness love? If I were to re-do my thoughts and actions of the day, how would I be more loving?

Spend as much or as little time on your practices as you wish. You are not judged by them. You are not judged by anything other than love. Many religious people believe they are judged by their words, thoughts, deeds, traits, and sins.

Since everything stems originally from love, they can only be judged by that.

Everyone has love in their heart, but it is not always evident. This is due to many factors that are being and have been studied by psychologists, medical professionals, clergy, lawyers, and advisors for centuries.

It is the fruit that falls from the tree metaphor. If it is an apple tree, an apple will fall. If someone is capable of feeling, expressing, and giving love and identifies with the love in their heart, love will be their fruit. If someone's heart is infected with hate, hate will likely be their fruit.

Here are a few factors that distort love: fear of death, fear of judgment, fear of worthlessness, fear of loneliness, fear of poverty, fear of rejection, and the fear of not being loved. Some say fear is the opposite of love. Love has no opposite and cannot be destroyed; however, fear can stifle one's ability to recognize, feel, express, and give others the love that is in their heart.

It is taking humanity a long time to recognize and return to the original state of love. It is happening and will continue to happen, though things might look worse on the outside during this process. The shift from love to hate and back and forth causes upheavals.

140

Your job is to recognize love in every way that you can. Starting with your daily activities, thoughts, and beliefs. Are they about love? This is the reflection to focus on at the end of each day.

The Value of Reading Scripture

"Watch your life and doctrine closely.
Persevere in them, because if you do, you
will save both yourself and your hearers."
1 Timothy 4:16 - New International Version

"All scripture is given by inspiration of God,
and is profitable for doctrine, for reproof, for
correction, for instruction in righteousness:"
2 Timothy 3:16 - King James Version

"Heaven and earth will pass away, but my
words will never pass away."
Matthew 24:35 - New English Translation

It is wise to learn what you can from scripture to make your life and your connection with God our Father be what you need. Physical life becomes more difficult when there is distance between your thoughts, words, and actions and your trust in God, your purpose, and eternal life.

Reading scripture may not sound attractive to some since many people object to certain parts and aspects of the Bible. However, the experience of confronting scripture and examining your own beliefs and turn-offs will strengthen you in ways that you are not able to conceive right now. You will hear others saying the same things you have thought. When that happens, you will be equipped to relate to where they are. You can offer assurance that they too will find peace with their spiritual, religious, and scriptural struggles.

No version of the Bible is more accurate or understandable than the others. There is much more to the creation, enactment, salvation, and ascension process than what humans currently understand. You will see many lights coming on soon. Many new interpretations and discoveries will occur within the next ten years.

Do not engage in arguments with people over biblical interpretations. I sympathize with those who are trying to understand the complexities of some of the scriptures and the messages that seem confusing, contrary, vengeful, and/or unloving. The predominant message I am here to deliver and reiterate is that of love, which originates with God our Father. Keep your focus on the scriptures that inspire Light and love in others and within your own self.

There are multiple human interpretations of every verse in the Bible. It would be best to avoid seeking consensus on which words mean what. Rather, seek out the heart of each message. Listen to your internal compass that always points to what is righteous and worthy

God's path is illuminated. When humans recognize the Light within and allow it to lead the way and shine for others, humanity finds its path to God's kingdom.

You are free to believe whatever you want to with whatever level of comprehension you have. When your heart is in the right place: you love God our Father; you love me, yourself, and humanity, this is all we need. Read and learn scripture so you have a point of reference that others may lean on and may be able to accept according to their level of comprehension.

Chapter 7 • 21st Century Topics

Bilocation and Mysteries of Science

"For where two or three are gathered together
in My name, there am I in the midst of them."
Matthew 18:20 - King James Version

"Then they reported what had happened on
the way, and how He was recognized by them
in the breaking of the bread. As they were
saying this, Jesus Himself stood among them
and said to them, "Peace be unto you." They
were terrified and frightened, and supposed
that they saw a spirit."
Luke 24:35-37 - Modern English Version

"Afterward Jesus appeared in a different form to
two of them while they were walking in the country."
Mark 16:12 - New International Version

"On the evening of that day, the first day of the
week, the doors being shut where the disciples
were, for fear of the Jews, Jesus came and stood
among them and said to them, "Peace be with you."
John 20:19 - Revised Standard Version

"Now all glory to God, who is able, through his
  mighty power at work within us, to accomplish
  infinitely more than we might ask or think."
  Ephesians 3:20 - New Living Translation

Imagine bilocation as a reality in the context of the infinite
possibilities of the universe. Then combine that with the
complexities of eternity and God, Creator of All That Is. How
can I, Jesus, exist in the minds and hearts of so many people
at one time?

Your scientists are still actively researching ways to
explain bilocation. There have been enough accounts of it to
warrant inquiry. They are also working on understanding
concepts such as the multi-verse and parallel universes.
Great scientific minds are working on quantum computing,
artificial general intelligence, underground farming, cloning,
and hybrid humans as well.

There are testimonies of life after death (near-death
experiences), the human soul, and other spiritual realities that
science cannot explain. It may take a while for the most
brilliant of your species to explain currently unaccepted
theories, hypotheses, and events, and convert them into
human advancements.

Here is a current quandary: What is consciousness and where is it located? Does it exist in the physical brain, the aura, or is it ethereal? Or...???

There are many mysteries to unravel, including those associated with my physical existence on Earth. If bilocation can be proven and accepted by a large percentage of the human populace, then, at some point other points of interest will be explained, including my origin, bloodline, and where I lived during my lifetime, especially the 12th through 30th years. I lived in all the places where my life and experiences were chronicled and recorded, by way of bilocation.

There are hints in scripture of this. Bits of information that were as strong and as clear as human consciousness could absorb in biblical times. There are biblical scholars today who are uncovering new information and figuring out how to explain it.

The Astral Mind of Creation

"But there is a spirit in man: and the inspiration
of the Almighty giveth them understanding."
Job 32:8 – King James Version

"But the Counselor, the Holy Spirit, whom
the Father will send in my name, will teach
you all things and remind you of everything
I have told you."
John 14:26 - Christian Standard Bible

The concept of the astral mind of creation refers to a particular access point of the infinitely creative mind of God, via what might be called astral travel. Accessing the astral plane is the most common way to engage creative-God-mind, so this is one reason it is called the astral mind of creation. The Holy Spirit is involved in this process.

There are other ways for humans to reach it as well. A human, or any life form for that matter, could never consciously connect with the totality of God because God is All That Is.

When one prays with an untethered heart, a call is made to the astral mind of creation. When one has a crossing experience, such as a near-death experience, an angelic visitation, a miracle, divine intervention, or an infusion of a

148

spark of Light and love, an instantaneous connection with the astral mind of creation is made. When any of these events occur, the person experiences a total surrender to love, a knowing, believing, understanding, and accepting

Those who undergo such a connection are often converted to a life of love and service. And yes, they might come under ridicule from those who cannot conceive of such experiences, or they might even be locked up in mental institutions. Many of the experiencers do not speak of them for this reason.

In the Christian world, even meditation and yoga are considered to be off base by some, perhaps many, Christians. Imagine what the early Jews/Christians went through and how they were persecuted, defamed, imprisoned, ridiculed, and even killed for their beliefs in the "new" thoughts of their days. Being a forerunner is not an easy role to play. However, it is the primary way that circumstances change, and consciousness is raised.

For consciousness to expand, someone within the current realm, the accepted mindset, must step out, experience, and then speak out. Otherwise, nothing advances, evolves, or grows. The manifest universe does not provide for stagnation. Not even the tiniest atomic particle rests.

For something physical to develop, morph, or transform, each particle involved undergoes a shift in vibrational frequency, change in spin, or rearranges itself to become a new life form.

Being a particle that vibrates at a slightly different frequency than those around it is temporarily uncomfortable until the new form emerges. It is similar to the discomfort of thinking differently and experimenting in non-Christian theologies while at the same time, exploring the steadfast beliefs and tenets of Christianity.

More on the concept of the astral mind of creation: The initiating point for connecting with this aspect of God-mind is recognizing, honoring, and pursuing the internal desire to create and explore. It is similar to the desire early humans had when they discovered how to harness fire, left the boundaries of their tribes, made boats to sail the seas, climbed mountains, etc.

It is also like a composer who sits down to write music, first hearing it in his/her mind or in a dream. Or an artist who sees an image in his/her mind and then paints it.

Mathematicians, scientists, and geniuses in many fields have reported how their new ideas and solutions came to them in a variety of ways, such as sitting in quietude, in the shower, while sleeping, or while engaged in a mundane task.

All these examples where the astral mind of creation was tapped were first stimulated by the deep desire to explore the limits and create/experience something new. This desire is what condenses the mental focus, thus connecting the human mind with the astral mind of creation.

Lightworkers, Those Who Magnify God's Light

> "You are the light of the world. A
> city that is set on a hill cannot be
> hidden."
> Matthew 5:14 - New King James Version

> "For with You is the fountain of life;
> In Your light we see light."
> Psalm 36:9 - New King James Version

The angel energy that many humans contain in part becomes much brighter due to their ability to grasp what is occurring in the world. It is not necessary to understand all the details; however, all is happening in accordance with a purpose and an unfolding that has been occurring over many millennia.

It is important for God's lightworkers to have access to information for the sake of self-awareness and to help others make it through changes that are and will be rapidly taking place. It is imperative to be aligned with God's purpose and to gain access to, not only personally accumulated knowledge but the knowledge of the ages. It is also important to strike a balance between traditional religious beliefs and 21st Century realities. Many have been deep into new ways of seeing the world, spirituality, and the unknown. Some have roots in the traditional ways of viewing right-wrong, heaven-hell, good-evil, Christian-nonChristian, etc. Many are here to help bridge the gap between the former traditional ways and the emerging ways of seeing and believing.

Those dedicated to God's Light must find balance. This is not work-life balance or finding ways to integrate family and community time into busy lives. This type of balance is the light-dark balance. It is the love-hate balance. And the infinite-finite balance that so many struggle to gain.

Be open to receiving help from other mortals, which is good. And be open to receiving help from other lightworkers, which serve us all. Pay heed to the following guidelines:

Context – The Need for Increased Light:

Human and animal freedoms and the earth's resources are being threatened in many ways, on many fronts. These existential threats are increasing daily. Reduced freedoms and greater destruction, resulting from extreme governmental domination and human greed, lust for power, the isolation of citizens, and selfishness is a 3D reality to be dealt with at the 3D level. The egregore of hate that feeds on suffering is growing and maturing exponentially.

Objectives:

- To reduce the power of the egregore of darkness that is influencing extremist political energy and domination energy, globally.
- To retain the dualistic nature of physical existence, with greater understanding of its purpose.
- To restore balance to the yin-yang of life, the light-dark, and love-hate balance.
- To bring peace and relief to those engaged in efforts to restore balance and dualism; those who are working behind the scenes and on the front lines.
- To still the waters of turbulence.
- To reduce fear and replace it with love and fearlessness.
- To help humanity realize that we are creating both positive and negative egregores with our thoughts and beliefs.
- To spread the message of love.
- To envision and live a life of peace, prosperity, joy, happiness, and love for all beings.

Common Practices:

- Quietude, prayer, meditation, and contemplation that support the mind and spirit.

- Breathwork, diet, movement, and rest that restore and support the physical body.
- Loving-kindness, acts of generosity, dedication to purpose, and modeling love that supports the human heart and the soul of humanity.
- Expressing, reaching out, sharing, and enlightening the collective mind of humanity, thus enabling the empowerment of the spirit of love, the egregore of Love

Potential Outcomes of the Work:

- Awareness by the masses as to the strength and power of human beings, as created by God our Father.
- Increased human awareness of the power and sovereignty of love.
- Cooperation of humans of all nationalities in rebuilding the health and beauty of the earth.
- Political agendas that benefit humanity and life are achieved without bloodshed and the destruction of natural resources.
- Liberation of those who are afflicted by and enslaved by the egregore of greed and the egregore of power.
- Liberation of those carrying out the will of the egregore of fear and suffering.

- Use of creative forces and energies to the benefit of the collective mind and the soul of humanity.
- Defeat of the egregores that enslave humanity and inflict terror on all lifeforms.
- Increase the number of souls who claim Jesus as Lord and those who return to the love and Light of God the Father.

Intuition

"Whatever the Lord God plans to do,
he tells his servants, the prophets."
Amos 3:7 - Contemporary English Version

Intuition is a guidance system that is an intricate combination of physical, inner soul, and angelic energy. Often when people say they have been guided by the Holy Spirit, their intuitive ability has been activated.

Intuition is innate in humans and is available to everyone who listens inwardly. Connecting with the Holy Spirit is possible for those who ask to be guided.

It is very tempting to observe others and pass judgment on them and their journeys. Everyone has their way of connecting with God our Father, albeit some are taking steep side trips and travel on slippery slopes. I understand that the perceived blindness of some and their perceived incapacity for love is concerning.

Notice that your concern is not so much about them as it is the threat they might pose to you, your loved ones, and your way of life.

You are best served by sorting out your beliefs, fears, reactions, and concerns regarding those who challenge the laws of your land and those who manipulate the masses.

157

Identify how people who seem to be separated from God affect you, your beliefs, and your spiritual mission.

What if someone came to you who genuinely fears that liberty is being taken away from the American people, that the laws of your country are unjust, the White House is corrupt, and the left is trying to destroy America? What if they told you they are being guided by God to fight for freedom? How would you respond? What would your intuition suggest? What would you do if you were to feel this stirring within yourself? There is much to be learned about self vs. others and the oneness of All That Is.

Reincarnation and Other Beliefs

Note to reader: *The Bible doesn't address reincarnation directly, which is why many traditional Christians understandably do not accept this concept. 21st Century Christianity acknowledges a wide array of spiritual beliefs that deeply endorse God's love.*

> "His breath goeth forth, he returneth to his earth; in that very day his thoughts perish."
> Psalm 146:4 – King James Version

> "Women received their dead raised to life again: and others were tortured, not accepting deliverance; that they might obtain a better resurrection:"
> Hebrews 11:35 - King James Version

> "If I have the gift of prophecy and can fathom all mysteries and all knowledge, and if I have a faith that can move mountains, but do not have love, I am nothing."
> 1 Corinthians 13:2 – New International Version

The concept of humans having only one life on earth is acceptable. The concept of reincarnation is also acceptable. There is no contest between these concepts for they both respond to the needs of the soul that embraces one or the other.

Remember, people believe only what they can believe. Many cannot even believe that their thoughts dictate their emotions which dictate their behavior. So how are we to expect that they can believe their actions and their circumstances in this life are influenced by previous lifetimes? It is too far of a stretch. People can only stay within reach of what they can grasp.

The truth is that all of life is occurring all the time in one measure. This is a difficult concept. So do not boggle your mind with it. Just stay committed to the purpose of life – which is to live. And stay tuned into the concept of love. Love is what life is all about, even though it does not always look like it through the lenses of earthly existence.

About Chakras

"You, Lord, are my lamp; the Lord turns
my darkness into light."
2 Samuel 22:29 - New International Version

"For thou wilt light my candle: the Lord
my God will enlighten my darkness."
Psalm 18:28 - King James Version

"The precepts of the Lord are right,
rejoicing the heart; The commandment
of the Lord is pure, enlightening the eyes."
Psalm 19:8 - New American Standard Bible 1995

The chakras are not a belief system. They are an explanation of an energy system (light) that you can access in your endeavors to increase your intuitive and inner-knowing capabilities; and strengthen your connection with the Divine.

Having clear, active chakras helps you to be internally focused so you can listen to and respond to the love of God our Father and the guidance of the Holy Spirit. It is important to make decisions regarding who to connect with and how you spend your time and physical energy. The feedback you receive when your chakras are attuned to your surroundings, and to other people, helps you in making such decisions.

When a conscious mind is open and unfocused, it is vulnerable to and can be overtaken by lower vibrational energies. This is why it is best to lift your mind to a higher state when you expand your consciousness during prayer, meditation, sleep, yoga, and chakra cleansing and activation.

Your intention is strong when you seek higher vibrations, guidance, and love.

It is best to protect your aura and chakras from interference, whether from an overt invasion like a negative spirit (egregore) trying to take over, or a covert invasion by erroneous thoughts, mistaken beliefs, or ungrounded fears, which cause spiritual vulnerability.

You have been advised that psychic training is necessary to hold off the evil (the egregore of hate) which is trying to permeate the consciousness of humanity, and this is true. It is necessary to be strong in mind and heart. If you are willing to focus on the chakra energies and calm your active mental state, it will be most beneficial, especially when you are responding to those who challenge your beliefs.

Do not engage in challenging conversations in a confrontational way. Address the hate energy that is circulating throughout Earth right now by invoking the available positive forces. The surge of hatred is throwing the balance of life's energies off.

Bring into focus the love that humanity longs for. Having clear, well-functioning energy centers (chakras) will assist you in staying grounded as you endeavor to love humanity.

Your Dreams

"For God speaks again and again, though
people do not recognize it. He speaks in
dreams, in visions of the night, when deep
sleep falls on people as they lie in their beds."
Job 33:14-15 - New Living Translation

In your dreams, the Holy Spirit provides truth, guidance and an undying faith in my love and the love of God. It develops your faith and your connections to the divine daily, even though you may not be consciously aware of your progress. Your dreams are filled with instances where you are learning truth and forbearance. You may not have conscious recall of your dream experiences every day, but they are very revealing of current times.

There is information being transmitted to you in your dreams. You do not need to have conscious recall of this information upon waking from the dream state, but it is helpful. Questions are being answered, the path is being shown, and the light is being turned up for you.

Develop a better practice for the rest-dream-awake cycle. I can also help clarify some of your lost ideas or misconceptions in the dream state, so it is best to fine-tune your receptivity.

Look forward. Pray. Listen inwardly. Pay attention to your dream world and the dreams of others close to you.

Align your consciousness with the continuance of life as is willed by God, Creator of All That Is. God-consciousness is a reality. Christ-consciousness is a reality. Your consciousness is a reality, as is the collective consciousness of humanity. It is all coming together.

Even though chaos is the new normal, have faith. Do not fret. All is good in God's time. You know this to be true.

Aliens

"There will be a time of distress such as
has not happened from the beginning of
nations until then."
Daniel 12:1 - New International Version

"For by Him all things were created that
are in heaven and that are in earth, visible
and invisible, whether they are thrones, or
dominions, or principalities, or powers.
All things were created by Him and for Him."
Colossians 1:16 - Modern English Version

"As they were walking along and talking
together, suddenly a chariot of fire and horses
of fire appeared and separated the two of them,
and Elijah went up to heaven in a whirlwind."
2 Kings 2:11 - New International Version
*(Note to Reader – Some say this sounds like an
alien encounter-abduction.)*

Many events are going to occur that will alter the sense of
reality and the beliefs of most people on Earth. There are very
few who will be able to contain or understand the strange
events and advances in technology that will be life-changing
for most humans and many animals on this planet.

166

As to whether there are aliens or not, the answer is yes, there are. They are alien to earthlings in the sense that nothing like them has been seen or experienced before this time. Are they from other planets, solar systems, galaxies, or other universes? I hesitate to answer directly as there is an unfolding that must take place. Think of infinite possibilities in an infinite universe.

The extraordinary truth will be held under the protection of Top Secret until governments can no longer exclude it from public knowledge. By then, people will have formed their own opinions and life-continuance strategies. Some information is already coming out of secrecy. You will have a conduit to truth that you are not quite prepared for at this time.

Be forewarned, fear within the masses will reproduce in magnitudes not previously known. It is best to continue to develop your ability to see things in a broad context rather than a tightly held definition of reality.

There is plenty in the biblical Book of Revelations that can forewarn people and open their minds to the supernatural aspects of life, especially physical-psycho-spiritual life, which is undergoing massive changes.

You will likely see, in the coming years, a trend for people to believe in the end of life on earth, God's reclamation, the apocalypse, rapture, my return, and all sorts of ideas. These will be fascinating and stressful times. Radical ideas will be fueled by fundamentalistic beliefs, fueled by fear. Expect great chaos.

What should the average human do? The immediate answer is to pray. For many this will not suffice. For you, it will. You believe that prayer is received and responded to, which it is.

However, do not necessarily pray that the end of times is averted. What is coming is not the total end, but for many, it will be. You will see belief systems crumbling and power grabs occurring at a magnified level. There are some who may be trying to bring on the apocalypse so that I will return and rapture will occur and they will be lifted to heaven. They are misguided.

The most interesting times will occur when people no longer rely on institutions, governments, or monetary systems to provide security and answers to problems.

That is when the human spirit will search for sustainable life. That is when the earth's resources will be severely plundered and destroyed and heavily relied upon as well. These events will not come to a full apex for 8-10 years, at least.

Much depends on the level of consciousness humanity can reach in the face of changing realities. Life and the future are in constant motion and subject to change in the moment.

Continue to pay attention to what is occurring in the world, especially in your land. Tensions are high. The stakes are high. The power centers are grasping for control while losing grip. Humans are realizing they have a God-given reservoir of strength to rely on. Hate is becoming more recognizable. All of these dynamics have an intense downside. However, there is a forthcoming upside.

21st Century Christmas

"This is how the birth of Jesus the Messiah
came about: His mother Mary was pledged
to be married to Joseph, but before they came
together, she was found to be pregnant
through the Holy Spirit."
Matthew 1:18 - New International Version

"One person esteems one day above another;
another esteems every day alike. Let each be
fully convinced in his own mind. He who
observes the day, observes it to the Lord;
and he who does not observe the day,
to the Lord he does not observe it."
Romans 14:5-6 - New King James Version

There are many options on how you spend your
Christmas holiday time. I have no prescribed rules or
suggestions about it. It is a time of year when people have a
good reason, or excuse, for getting together with friends and
loved ones. Adding the religious aspects of my birth is
optional. The traditions and holidays are fine with me either
way.

The message I prefer that people focus on during the
Christmas season is the message of God's eternal love.

Many believe they can fall out of favor with God our Father if they do not follow religious rules and traditions. If (when) they break the Ten Commandments or they sin and then sin again, they might feel defeated.

To experience, express, and share love is the ultimate accomplishment. This is what Christmas is all about; giving gifts of love to every being you encounter.

Chapter 8 • The Big Picture Forward
Our Mission, Our Source

"Now this is our boast: Our conscience testifies
that we have conducted ourselves in the world,
and especially in our relations with you, with
integrity and godly sincerity. We have done so,
relying not on worldly wisdom but on God's grace."
2 Corinthians 1:12 - New International Version

"What a wonderful God we have—he is the
Father of our Lord Jesus Christ, the source of
every mercy, and the one who so wonderfully
comforts and strengthens us in our hardships
and trials. And why does he do this? So that
when others are troubled, needing our sympathy
and encouragement, we can pass on to them this
same help and comfort God has given us."
2 Corinthians 1:3-4 – Living Bible

People believe whatever they choose to believe
regardless of their sources. This is the beauty of free will, free
thought, and free choice. It is challenging when people do not
check their sources or seek the truth of what they are being
asked to believe.

Impacting human consciousness is the goal of our mission: to lift the collective mind into the Light and fill the collective heart with love. That is all we are focused on. With no end goal in mind. We are not on a mission that has a reward to be won or a victory lap to be run.

We are a part of the tide that flows in and out of the realm of human consciousness. It is not right when the tide is high, and it is not wrong when it is low. We are focusing on the point where the tide changes direction. We are engaged in the shift from low tide to high tide, and our goal is to support the shift with greater love and awareness.

There is no battle between good and evil as absolutes. However, there is a balancing act. We are in it together only because you have chosen to be a part of it according to your own spiritual mission.

I am working with you to help lighten the consciousness of humankind with love, thus reducing the power of hate and destruction occurring on Earth.

My teaching model is designed to bring your awareness to a higher level of love. I engage you in encouraging your fellow humans to reach this awareness. It is not a model with steps 1, 2, and 3. However, it has an intended purpose, process, and potential outcome.

I want you to be familiar with scripture so you can support those who are called to the mission of universal love. We are not restricted to Christian or Jewish religious beliefs. There are many prophets and teachers who do not align with a particular denomination, sect, or religion. They occasionally, or often, refer to and defer to messages and passages in the Bible, as well as other holy texts.

Our source is God our Father, who is far too great to be confined to a single religion. The religion of love and forgiveness is God's.

You never need to fear, as long as you trust in the Lord and know that our Father is the Source of All That Is. Our Source extends beyond the human belief in scarcity. Our source is with us always and forever. Forever extends beyond the human capacity to imagine time.

We are all in this together, which is why we need the type of communication that assists people in recognizing truth and love, deception and hatred. Many messages are being transmitted to the collective mind, creating much turmoil in the world today. My mission, and yours by choice, is the mission of clarity, love, and peace.

God's Original Intent and Free Will

"You were called to freedom, brothers and
sisters; only don't let this freedom be an
opportunity to indulge your selfish impulses,
but serve each other through love."
Galatians 5:13 - Common English Bible

"Let the wicked one abandon his way and
the sinful one his thoughts; let him return
to the Lord, so he may have compassion on
him, and to our God, for he will freely forgive."
Isaiah 55:7 - Christian Standard Bible

The ability of humans to love and live with each other in a
mutually supportive way was the original intent and design
[Eden]. The inclusion of free will in God's plan is where it
became an experiment in true love. With free will comes the
truth. Would you want to be married to someone because
they have to be with you or because they want to be with you?
Would you want your offspring to visit you after they have
established their own homes because they are compelled by
guilt or because they want to?

God did not create robots, a non-thinking species, or
subjects that are forced to comply. God created a companion
species with God-like attributes such as the abilities to

imagine, design, choose, and create. This is why God gave free will to humankind. Humans are sorting out their powers right now.

The outcomes humanity produces from its trials and tribulations and self-imposed battles will be interesting and enlightening. God is not forcing any particular outcome but has high hopes and trust that humanity will live up to God's original intent.

The current upsets, drama, back-stabbing, name-calling, and undermining are the paths humanity is taking to find its true self. Humanity is in its puberty. When a youngster discovers it can defy its parents, make its own choices, run free, and design its own future, things can get messy and chaotic.

Free will choices do not always work out well. The consequences are often greater than anticipated. Freedom is not quite what it seemed like it would be. Growth and maturity eventually ensue.

Moving from being on one side of the fence where everything is provided and the boundaries are clear, to stepping into open space where anything can happen is often frightening for humans. Many have experienced this and most did not feel safe and secure.

Breaking free of constraints is a blessing in disguise. It is scary and simultaneously provides the strength and confidence needed to face current and future uncertainties and difficulties.

As you discover the interconnectedness of All That Is, you will eventually accept whatever shows up, without the need to judge, understand, or explain it.

You will be in the state that has been described as the Tao, Nirvana, Heaven, Awakened, Enlightened, or Ascended, to list a few descriptors. This is the point where one's free will and God's will mesh.

You do not need to leave the physical realm to experience this. This state of being is wordless. It is mind-blowing, which is why some people who experience it might not fit into society and might be deemed as untethered to reality.

There is no worldly benefit to reaching this state. There is no rush. It is fine to exist in the duality of separation where boundaries, labels, distinctions, and beliefs are important.

Whether to mistreat, kill, or accept each other over resources and cultural differences is where humanity is currently fixated. Some are becoming aware of the consequences of free will. Others are operating with self-will and self-survival, which is different from free will. Being a slave to self is not freedom. It is slavery in a subtle form because the oppressor is not visible in most cases.

Destroying each other emotionally, mentally, physically, spiritually, or politically is a choice that presents itself to humanity over and over until people figure out a way to live together in cooperation and love, which is the original intent of God-Source.

Do not fret. You do not need to understand or have answers for what you are seeing on the news and around you. Your role is to enhance the consciousness of those in your life with love, if they are open to it. If not, you can trust they will eventually find their path to love. You are not responsible for their free will choices.

The weight of the world is not on your shoulders. When you hear that the world is an illusion, you can rely on that concept. In truth, only love is everlasting. This is not easy to understand because the word "love" does not sufficiently translate into causal reality.

Much will be discovered, embraced, and accomplished when humanity recognizes its ability to exercise collective free will. Right now, most humans are unconsciously using the power of free will. When free will is conscious and deliberate at the individual level, much will change.

When multitudes of people exercise this gift, mass consciousness shall expand. This is when God our Father smiles upon humanity and the angels celebrate.

Purpose and the Possible

"And Jesus looking upon them said to them,
With men this is impossible; but with God
all things are possible."
Matthew 19:26 – American Standard Version

"I pray that out of his glorious riches he may
strengthen you with power through his Spirit
in your inner being, so that Christ may dwell
in your hearts through faith. And I pray that you,
being rooted and established in love, may have
power, together with all the Lord's holy people,
to grasp how wide and long and high and deep
is the love of Christ, and to know this love that
surpasses knowledge—that you may be filled
to the measure of all the fullness of God."
Ephesians 3:16-19 - New International Version

Turn to scripture for comfort. Search for passages that address God's forgiveness of humanity, including yourself. Bring the written word that gives you solace into your heart and hold on to it when your inter-personal communications become tense. Trust that you can overcome your tendencies to react inappropriately. You will learn the cues and skills needed to navigate in a tumultuous world.

Intending that your soul remains obedient to God our Father will help your personality-self remain attuned to your soul's intention of healing and spiritual growth.

You are in the right place at the right time for the right reasons. Do not doubt the purposefulness of your life and the value of your experiences. Your self-awareness will increase with each opportunity that presents itself.

Someone can heal completely and become trusting, free, and happy after having been abused, traumatized, misunderstood, and neglected. With God our Father, all things are possible.

Personal healing and transformation are not only possible but are required for the ascension process to be completed. Every soul is on a path of ascension, returning to our Father.

Some souls do not appear to relate to higher consciousness or the love of our Father. However, they are connected and loved. Their role is that of demonstration and display. They provide a mirror for others to see what they reject in themselves.

Be a model soul in the process of reuniting with God our Father to serve others and model love. Your personal healing will be evidence to others that the love of God our Father is real and can be relied upon.

Strengthen Your Soul

"For length of days, and years of life,
and peace, will they add to thee. Let
not kindness and truth forsake thee:
Bind them about thy neck; Write them
upon the tablet of thy heart: So shalt
thou find favor and good understanding
in the sight of God and man."
Proverbs 3:2-4 – American Standard Version

"Do not be anxious about anything, but
in every situation, by prayer and petition,
with thanksgiving, present your requests
to God. And the peace of God, which
transcends all understanding, will guard
your hearts and your minds in Christ Jesus."
Philippians 4:6-7 - New International Version

Keep a journal of evidence to prove to yourself that love is growing stronger even when the hearts of people appear to be heavy or misguided. Whenever you come across a song, a passage in scripture, a post on social media, a video, or a comment someone makes that indicates the love of God is prevailing, write it down in this journal. Or perhaps you would prefer to keep it on your phone. This will strengthen your soul and encourage those who need it.

All human emotions are accepted and understood. You may have your shame, but it is not necessary. I am quite familiar with the range of intensity and expression that arises from one's core feelings. It is helpful to identify them. You have made progress since your early years when you did not know what you were thinking or how you were feeling. Your soul gains strength with each challenge in life.

Recall the story you read to your children about fortunate and unfortunate events. Each fortunate event led to an unfortunate outcome; each unfortunate outcome led to a fortunate event.

Recall the account of the slave woman you read about who experienced great suffering. She was able to find the good in her pain as she discovered a reservoir of strength within herself.

It is not possible to judge when things are going well or badly while you are amid current events. What may look like a disaster could be the best thing that happens. And vice versa. Hold this in mind.

The purpose of experiences on earth, good or bad, is for God to manifest in humanity. God created the world, not to let it spin out of control, not to pit humans against each other, but to love his creations, no matter what they do with the life he gave them. Those who resist and reject God's purpose are given a chance to redeem themselves, repeatedly.

Speak as freely as you wish of the guidance you receive from the Holy Spirit. Do not fear embarrassment if "unfortunate" results occur when you act upon this guidance. Honor the "fortunate" aspects of each experience, no matter what the event looks like on the outside.

Continue to follow my guidance and God's love, as delivered by the Holy Spirit. This is your soul-strengthening exercise.

How another person reacts to the good news of life after death, eternity with God our Father, and the possibility of having faith while experiencing fear, is not up to you. It is up to them. You might feel that you occasionally fail to speak of God's love in a way that moves others to accept. But five years later, they might recall what you said and act on it, not even remembering that you planted the seed.

There is no set pattern to how individuals receive God's word, by whom, or when. Your task is to speak as freely and as confidently as you care to, with no parameters as to when, how, what to say, or where. As you confirm your trust in God's love, your soul is strengthened, whether others are influenced or not.

Trust God, rely on scripture, and trust yourself. You will not let yourself or your loved ones down. Of this you can be assured. Find solace in nature and accept your truth.

All is well.

Love, Jesus

• • •

"Under my authority, the copyright of this material belongs to anyone who takes part or all of this publication to heart and shares it with others in any honest format, without modification, subject to language translations." Jesus

Backstory

As a baby, I was christened in a protestant church, but I can't tell you if it was Presbyterian, Methodist, or Episcopalian. We went to all three. My mother had a deep unrest in her soul, and we moved around a lot. For me, the church, whichever one we attended, was the anchor in my unstable life.

My parents divorced when I was four years old, due to my father's infidelity and my mother's rejection of the double standard of the times. What kept me, my siblings, and our mother together as a family during the next eleven years of my life was the church. What kept me together personally was the song, "*Jesus Loves Me*." It gave me great comfort in turbulent times.

When I was a sophomore in high school my mom became a Bahai'. If you're not familiar with the Bahai' faith, it's a Middle Eastern religion that is a compassionate, non-violent counter-religion to Islam. The Bahai' faith is monotheistic (one true God) and respects all the major love-based religions of the world, Christianity included.

My mother had been experiencing social condemnation and hypocrisy in the churches we attended while raising five children and undergoing several divorces along the way. She wanted to disassociate with the church, though she had a deep and sincere love for Christ. When a friend introduced her to the Bahai' faith, she found her home and was finally at peace with God, Christ, and the Christian religion.

I, on the other hand, was very angry with my mother for her choice. We moved to a small town in Florida where her Bahai' friend and his wife lived. It had 4,000+- year-round residents with an additional 6,000+- snowbirds. This tiny town had one school for all 12 grades, many churches, and no synagogue. There was very little tolerance for non-Christian views. And here we were, one of two families connected to the Bahai' faith. My social life was torn apart. I wanted to go to church with my new Christian friends but doing so seemed disloyal to my mom's path. I abandoned all religion at that point.

This was in 1967 when the hippy movement was cranking up. Organized religion was being rejected by young people, along with most major institutions. I adopted many of the values and social messages of the new age, many of which were spiritual in nature, such as non-violence, peace, love, and anti-war.

My spiritual focus shifted from "Jesus loves me" to "There's got to be a better way." I joined my first lightworkers meditation group a couple of years later. Our mission was to

188

send Light and Love to the whole world. I followed my winding spiritual path for many years, including teaching Sunday School at a Unitarian Universalist church and taking five levels of Shambhala Buddhist meditation training. I attended Quaker meetings and random services at the Science of Mind church for a couple of years. I even took one of their courses.

I stayed away from traditional Christianity and institutional religion. In late 2019 through early 2020, with my brother John's help, I put together a YouTube video series called *Awakening Your Everyday Wisdom.* Church was not a part of my life then.

One evening in late 2020, everything changed. Exhausted from my caregiver responsibilities (my husband was in the final stages of his life) and still in the 5-year recovery period from cancer myself, I spent my off-time relaxing.

I sat quietly in my room, meditating, contemplating, listening to calming music, and smoking legal cannabis, which my very conservative oncologist recommended.

One night, in this relaxed state, I saw the face of Jesus. It filled the entire room. His face was gentle and loving and the image only lasted a few seconds. But I was shocked by it. I didn't take cannabis for several days after that, thinking I must have overdone it.

The memory of the face of Jesus would not leave my mind. I began to pray nightly, welcoming Jesus into my heart and asking him to take me into his heart.

I moved to Beaufort, South Carolina at the end of 2021, shortly after my husband passed away. Moving here was a divinely guided event. About six months afterwards I had a vision of being baptized in a river. It was a very clear image and was rather disturbing. I didn't continue taking regular cannabis after I moved to South Carolina, so I knew that wasn't the cause of this vision.

Even though I had accepted Jesus into my life, I had no intention of becoming a Christian again. And baptism was out of the question. I was very disappointed in the way Christianity was being distorted for political reasons. I'm still disturbed by this. Despite my resistance, the vision of being baptized did not leave me.

During the spring of 2022, I kept having recurring thoughts about it. I pondered what full immersion would be like.

At first, I didn't take these thoughts seriously, given the certainty of my spiritual mission as a lightworker and spiritual mentor, but not as a Christian. At that point, I was studying online at Edgar Cayce's Atlantic University to obtain my certificate in Spiritual Mentoring. I never doubted my path of supporting others on their spiritual journeys and helping other earth angels and lightworkers complete their missions.

My feelings about this recurring inspiration to get baptized included confusion, anger, resistance, and curiosity. I'd been aligned with the new-age movement for my entire adult life. The notion of getting baptized was contrary to my chosen path. But I couldn't seem to shake it.

I entertained the idea of asking a friend to dunk me in a river in Jesus' name. That seemed like a cop-out but was preferable to anything formal. The alternative idea I considered was to check out a local Baptist church as I knew that Baptists believed in full immersion. While I was grappling with all this, my internal nudges, defiant resistance, and strong feelings would not go away.

Shortly after receiving this vision, I made a new friend at the chiropractor's office, who was, ironically, a member of The Baptist Church of Beaufort. I asked her if I could be baptized at her church without joining the church. She referred me to the pastor.

After meeting with him, I had mixed feelings. He was very open and did not try to convince me to join the church so I could get baptized. He gave me several options to consider

191

and a book to read that had a chapter about a Baptist's view of baptism.

That was June 15, 2022, before my weekly conversations with Jesus started. I was upset, angry, and confused as I was driving home from my appointment with the pastor. I went inside and immediately sat down to write in my journal to help me sort things out.

I asked questions and, much to my surprise, received answers. The first part of this conversation went as follows:

Anne – "Dearest Jesus, do you want me to be baptized?"

Jesus – "Yes"

Anne – "Why?!!!"

Jesus – "I ask you to come to me in heart, mind, spirit, and body."

Anne – "But why through baptism?"

Jesus – "Because I know you. And I know how much it would mean to you and how transformative it would be."

Anne – "I feel confused because I have given up on traditional religion and I'm really disappointed in the way Christianity is being distorted these days."

Jesus – "Me too."

Anne – "But if I'm baptized, it would be a step backward, into the confusion and distortion of Christianity that I divorced many years ago."

Jesus – "Yes…… "I want you to have a guardrail, a pipeline, and a conduit to truth via a personal and publicly displayed connection, conviction, and resurrection."

This conversation went on for another page or so in my journal. Three months later, 9-19-22, I was invited to a spiritual mentoring session with Jesus (see my dream note at the beginning of this book).

After ten months of praying, journaling, having intermittent conversations with the pastor, much soul searching, and having these weekly conversations with Jesus, I joined the church and was baptized by full immersion.

At this point in my journey, I can offer assurance that all is well in God's time. I've recently become a Stephen Minister at The Baptist Church of Beaufort, with the mission of listening to, being with, spiritually caring for, and encouraging people who are experiencing grief, loss, and heavy challenges.

I struggled quite a bit with the thought of coming out and telling people about my experiences with Jesus and publishing this book. I didn't want it to appear that I was trying to capitalize on Jesus' wisdom since I am a certified spiritual mentor myself. I sincerely believe everything here came from him and I feel the importance of sharing his wisdom. I have been, and still am, worried that people will call me a crackpot, a shyster, a fraud, or worse.

As a human being, I don't have the ability to speak these divine concepts from my own understanding. I am not purporting to be a prophet. I'm more like a messenger for those who want to hear. Though the words are mine, I acknowledge Jesus as the source of them. He provided the wisdom in this book.

Peace and love, *Anne*

•　•　•

Personal Journaling Questions

Note to reader: For context, please refer to the chapters and their topic sections:

Chapter 1 - God our Father

- What about you? Do you value your life as a slave or a child might? Take these questions into contemplation: What value do you place on your life and for what reasons?

Chapter 1 - Accepting God's Love

- Why do you think you are here on earth in human form subject to human conditions?

Chapter 2 - The End of Times

- In what ways do you choose love?

Chapter 3 - Current Events and Hot Topics

- How will you endure the challenges and the violence you see on the news?
- How will you manage your elder years if/when the economic structures of your country are challenged and dismantled?

- If you depend on a government program, how will you support yourself if this program is discontinued?

Chapter 3 - Past, Future, and Present

- What are you thinking, believing, and doing right now, with your current understanding, desires, and capabilities?

Chapter 3 - Fear of the Future and Faith

- What do you want to have happen? What are you praying for? Once these answers are clear, the creative forces of God will coalesce to bring your desires into your physical experience.
- Recognize the effects fear has on your body and emotions. When you are afraid, answer the same questions previously asked: What do you want to have happen regarding the fear you are experiencing? What are you praying for?
- When you are concerned about your security, answer these same questions. What do you want to have happen? What are you praying for?

The next steps are the same for each person regardless of gender or age:

- Put your questions, desires, and prayers into clear words, in writing.
- Recall the times when fear dominated your thoughts, beliefs, and behaviors.
- Compare what you fear to what you pray for. Is the source of your fear the doubt that you will not receive what you want and need? Is it a lack of trust in the Lord? Is it believing what appears to be the fearful truth in the physical world rather than believing in the power of your intentions and prayers?
- Deciding how to respond to fear-producing events is the key. Having a personal fear-response plan makes the difference in whether you are living a fear-based life or a prayer-based life.

Chapter 4 - Painful Memories
- How can you retain your important memories and release the painful, disabling ones?

Chapter 4 - Worry and How to Deal with It
- How can you best use past experiences for learning and growing and stay present to your current and future situations without worrying?

- Put the "all-in-your-mind" conversations aside and count your blessings, strengths, spiritual progress, and your righteous accomplishments. You might have a long list to compile.
- Distinguish what is worth your concern from what is not.

Chapter 4 - The Shadow Side and God's Love

- What is your reward for facing your fears and living in your true reality?
- What do you want that you're afraid you will never have? Do you long to express your true self and experience freedom?

Chapter 4 - Needs, Desires, Gratitude, and Freedom

- What is required for you to truly experience gratitude?
- What do you need and/or want now, which is what you would be grateful for in the future?

Chapter 5 - Positive Shift in Consciousness

- Live in the present without focusing on the issues and concerns of the present. How do you accomplish this?
- What issues and concerns of your present were created by the consciousness, words, beliefs, fears, worries, and actions of your past?

Chapter 5 - Changing Your Life

- Magnify your recurring thoughts, beliefs, and assumptions so you can learn from them. Observe how they affect the qualities and emotional aspects of your life.
- Exercise your power to change any dissatisfying or limiting states of being you are experiencing.
- From there decide which perceptions fit your highest intentions and which ones need adjustment.

Chapter 5 - Discernment, Focus, and Trust

- How do you approach and integrate love into your human experience?

Chapter 5 - Living Life

- How do you describe your best life?
- What concerns do you have that make you want to be in the driver's seat?
- Look at your list and see what you can release to lighten your load so that your landing is not a hard one.

Chapter 5 - The Value of Your Life

- What is at the foundation of your perception of the value of your life?

- What makes you valuable, important, worthy, or significant?

- Magnify your recurring thoughts, beliefs, and assumptions so you can learn from them. How do they affect the qualities and emotional aspects of your life?

- Create a vision of the value you desire your life to have. Once that is clear in your consciousness and while you are in the state of flow, you will be able to recognize what fits your vision and what does not.

- You will learn more as you practice awareness of your thoughts and states of being. For example: stressed-out, fun-loving, uneasy, easy-go-lucky, longing, etc.

Chapter 6 - Religious Information

- In what ways did you love today?

- How and where did you witness love?

- If you were to re-do your thoughts and actions of the day, how would you be more loving?

Chapter 8 - Strengthen Your Soul

- Keep a journal of evidence to prove to yourself that love is growing stronger even when the hearts of people appear to be heavy or misguided.

- Whenever you come across a song, a passage in scripture, a post on social media, a video, or a comment someone makes that indicates the love of God is prevailing, write it down in this journal. This will strengthen your soul and encourage those who need it.

- Go deep within your heart to discover your true motives (for sharing your spiritual experiences and beliefs with others). There you will find inner confidence and strength in your soul.

• • •

Credits

<u>Jesus</u> – Spiritual Mentor

<u>Anne Neal-Dugdale</u> – Certified Spiritual Mentor - Having been called by Jesus a few years ago and as a student of his love, this book is a compilation of the many sessions she had as a mentee of Jesus. Anne humbly offers this 21st-century approach to fellow Christians, travelers in other religions, and the spiritual/non-religious. Contact Anne at: new21stCenturyChristianity@gmail.com or annenealdugdale@substack.com

<u>Pam Muller</u> – Spiritual Director – Pam has been a trusted partner in Anne's experience of having dialogues with Jesus. Pam specializes in dream work, working one-on-one with clients and in groups, using her dream expertise and empathic listening and reflection skills. Her work and contact information: SweetGeorgiaPam.com and on social media @SweetGeorgiaPam – sweetgeorgiapam@gmail.com

<u>Landon Collins</u> – Senior Pastor – The Baptist Church of Beaufort - Landon counseled Anne throughout her return to Christianity and during the many months of her spiritual mentoring sessions with Jesus. He baptized her in April of 2023. – lcollins@bcob.org

<u>Bill Hardee</u> – Retired Baptist Pastor – served at six churches and as Chair of the Religion Department at Tift College, adjunct Professor at S.W.B.T.S. (a Baptist Seminary), a parochial school Headmaster, and as a Hospice Chaplain. He also served as an adjunct professor of the New and Old Testament at Mercer University.

<u>Dr. Constance T. Johnson, J.D. PhD</u> – Consultant and Proofreader Constance is an ordained minister, teacher, author, and spiritual adventurer.

<u>John Arthur Neal</u> – Compositor and Advisor – John has written nine novels, two novellas, 21 short stories, and several screenplays. John was instrumental in assembling and publishing this book.

Bibliography

Quoted verses were excerpted from the website: *biblegateway.com*. **Bible Gateway** is a searchable online tool hosting more than 200 versions of the Bible in over 70 languages that you can freely read, research, and reference anywhere. Including a library of audio Bibles, mobile apps, devotionals, email newsletters, and other free resources, **Bible Gateway** equips you not only to read the Bible but to understand it.

Mythical Encyclopedia, LLC., which preserves the rich tapestry of global mythology and researches a variety of cultures. *mythicalencyclopedia.com*

The Theosophical Society in America Additional information is available at *theosophical.org*.

Egregores: The Occult Entities That Watch Over Human Destiny by Mark Stavish and James Wasserman, 2018, Inner Traditions/Bear & Company

With great gratitude to God our Father,
Jesus Christ, and the Holy Spirit.

● ● ● ●

Current and Upcoming Offerings in the Series

An Approach to
21st Century Christianity

Volume 1 • Spiritual Mentoring with Jesus
A composite of compassionate and direct insights from Jesus to address and navigate human concerns and fears inherent in our modern-day challenges.

> Printed Book • $16.99 plus shipping
> eBook • $8.99 download
> Audiobook (Coming soon)

Volume 2 • Conversations with Mary Magdalene
Inspiration for developing Universal Feminine Consciousness and gifting humanity with Divine Feminine Love. This is one of hundreds of books about Mary Magdalene, the Apostle of the Apostles.

> Printed Book • $16.99 plus shipping
> eBook • $8.99 download
> Audiobook (Coming soon)

Volume 3 • Daily Messages • Personal Journal
Impactful quotes from Jesus (Volume 1) and inspirational quotes about love from Mary Magdalene (Volume 2). This journal is for your explorations, reflections, and insights on the quotes spanning 365 days.

> Printed Journal • $21.99 plus shipping

Volume 4 • Is It Love? Is It Hate? • Personal Journal
This journal includes Jesus' distinctions of love and hate with space for you to reflect on their meaning and effects in your life.

> Printed Journal • $16.99 plus shipping

Volume 5 • *Dreams from the Divine*
God our Father, Jesus, the Holy Spirit, our higher
consciousness, and spirit guides often communicate with us
through dream images and scenarios. This book contains a
variety of the author's dreams, reflections, prayers, and
guidance from the Divine, and includes dream recollection and
interpretation tips for you to use with your dreams.

> Printed Book • $16.99 plus shipping (Coming April 2025)
> eBook (Coming April 2025)

All of these books and eBooks can be purchased from
https://shop.ingramspark.com

Simply search for the subtitle you're interested in:

- *Spiritual Mentoring with Jesus*
- *Conversations with Mary Magdalene*
- *Daily Messages*
- *Is It Love? Is It Hate?*
- *Dreams from the Divine*

Thank you for your participation in this mission of love.

•   •   •   •   •